kate magic wood

recipes for the revolution

Raw Magic

Uni-verso

Raw magic can heal the planet –
Eating this way can save the day!
This is food as art,
Food from the heart.
Packed with love,
It's always enough.
Makes you shine,
Like a being divine.
Fills you with truth
This book is the proof!
So feed your cells with gourmet bliss,
Cos you've never tasted anything quite like this.

Printing

Printed in The United Kingdom of Great Britain by:
Rawcreation Ltd (www.rawcreation.com)
Millennium House, Gapton Hall Road, Great Yarmouth, Norfolk NR31 0NL, UK

Disclaimer

This book is sold for information purposes only. Neither the author nor the publisher will be held accountable for the use or misuse of the information contained in this book. This book is not intended as medical advice, because the author and publisher are not medical doctors and do not recommend the use of medicines to achieve ecstatic bliss or to alleviate health challenges.

Because there is always some risk involved, the author, publisher and/or distributors of this book are not responsible for any adverse effects or consequences resulting from the use of any recipes, suggestions or procedures described hereafter.

Acknowledgements

Wow, so many amazing people in my life. These are the friends who loved, supported, motivated and inspired me while I was writing this book.

Chris, the best ex-husband ever; Sir Reuben the Shanti, Sir Ethan the Funny, Sir Zachary the Flubber; Doxtor Shazzie Ecstasist Vageniyummy & Madam Evie Popple Cake; raw goddess lovers Alxxx, Love Sky Dancer, Jonny 4 Peace, TS, badbad-chad; raw goddess Holly; rawvolutionaries Green Gela, Joel the cosmic cacao kid, Suki Xocolati Zoe, Rawchelle, Matt Monarch, Daniela Vanilla; yummy mummies Lucidia, Tara and Heidi; magic mates Twinkel, Lucifer, Jo Faerie, Smiley Jo, Mee, Pipparoni, Linus, Lisa & family, Cosmic Chris Wheatgrass, Galactic Guy, Shaman Sean & family; raw livers Peter, Mark 1 and Mark 2, Amy and Lucy; the Guarana bar for getting me through the boring bits near the end; all the supersuper djs and musicians whose music accompanied the writing of this book – Gilles, Benji B, BTS radio, Marc Mac and 4Hero, Simbad, Ben Westbeech, Karizma; the pioneers at Tree Harvest, Creative Nature, Detox Your World, and Of The Earth.

I would also like to thank all the people who made it hard for me, who told me I couldn't do it, who bitched about me, who ripped me off, who didn't believe in me, who stood in my way. You made me strong, you made me who I am today, you made me work even harder to show the world how much love I had inside of me to share, and for that I am truly grateful.

Contents

When people start eating raw foods and superfoods magic starts to happen. I can't fully explain it because it's to do with waking up to a magical state of consciousness that's beyond words. Thank heavens for that! Yet Kate so beautifully explains in this book how to create delicious food that will help you towards this state of consciousness. This quality of information about superfoods has never been brought together in this way before.

High quality raw foods and superfoods actually nourish the right hemisphere of the brain. This is where we are creative, inspired, inspirational, connected, loving, sensual and intuitive. As we shift towards this way of being and doing so the world will shift: from one of left-brain dominance that creates an artificial world to one of right-brain genius-like co-creation and all the joy, love and bliss that it brings.

Kate is deeply committed to world change – not planning it as such, but being it in every moment. "Be the change you wish to see in the world" by Gandhi is one of her favourite quotes. Where else can change happen but within ourselves?

Kate is a real person with three young sons, a house to run, work to do, food to make and a budget to manage – all within the ever-decreasing 24 hours per day. This makes this book even more special. The extra energy she has for projects like this book is from living, eating and thinking the way she does. She reveals how you can do the same in this book.

We can all bring magic into our lives, whatever our circumstances. Kate meets life – and its challenges – with such a beautiful smile on her face, and even sometimes with pink frilly knickers! I can almost hear her infectious laugh as I peruse the pages of Raw Magic.

Kate's recipes are legendary; I love the way she focuses on the goodies! And believe me, even salads are goodies at Kate's house. This book demonstrates how fun, easy and delicious being healthy really is. It will inspire masses of people to make the change. If we are what we eat then of course we want to eat delicious, mouth-watering, gorgeous, tasty, vibrant food.

I recently spent an extraordinarily uncomfortable and disturbed night sleeping half-on and half-off a bean bag in Kate's lounge. After I woke up laughing about it, we agreed "we've changed our brain chemistry now to a point where we can enjoy anything that happens". Revolutionary talk!

Kate is truly a visionary. She explains that it's so much about raw food, and so much more than raw food. Getting the right nutrients and energies from food helps us to be multidimensional beings in this three dimensional world. Who knows where all this will lead? Are you ready for the ride of your life?

One of my favourite quotes of Kate's is "You can't be against things, only for things". Well, I'm for Kate and Raw Magic and everyone reading this book, wherever it takes us.

With much love

Holly Paige
Raw Magic Tantric Divine Mother Love Goddess

www.oceanwavevibrations.com

What is Raw Magic?

1

There are some foods that have the power to change your life.

When you eat certain foods your body is in heaven, your cells start singing, your mind becomes ecstatic. "Yes," they cry in unison, "Yes, these are the foods that I have been waiting for. These are the foods that I have been craving, that my body has been missing my whole life."

Sometimes it is a particular nutrient you have been lacking. But more often with these foods it is their synergistic properties. They have a magical energy that comes not only from the nutritional combination they contain but from the way they are grown, the lands they are from, their history. Many of them are sacred plants in their countries of origin.

There are many amazing foods that I don't class as superfoods in this book, though other people do: vegetables like broccoli, kale and cucumbers; fruits like cranberries, blueberries and grapefruit; sprouts like lentils, sunflower or alfalfa. I was tempted to include avocados and olives, buckwheat and oats, all foods I eat on a daily basis. But these are foods that most of us are familiar with, and if you are not then there are plenty of books out there that do cover them.

This book is about the new breed of superfoods that are unique to the West in the 21st century. Never before have we had access to such a wide variety of plant foods. Some of them we are accustomed to in different forms, like cacao; others have been around for a few decades now, like spirulina; some are widely known in their country of origin, but novel to the UK, like goji berries; and some others are utterly brand new to us, like purple corn.

When I was a child, avocados and kiwis were considered exotic; now they are standard fare in every shopping basket. I believe that such is the potency and vitality of the foods in this book that as people catch on to them, they are going to revolutionise the way we eat, shop and live.

These foods are transformative foods

Eating such high-potency foods changes the very nature of our reality. They affect our consciousness and raise our energetic level to a degree that has profound implications on all areas of our lives.

It is not possible to eat these foods on a daily basis and not feel altered. We live in a culture which is intrinsically false: fuelled on junk food, media lies, false gods and political whores, we have forgotten how to be our true selves. These foods help us realign, connect with who we really are, and tune into our higher selves.

It becomes increasingly hard not to live in our power when we eat this way, and this can be a difficult adjustment to make in a world where the individual is fundamentally disempowered.

Revealing our inner core is usually painful: as we let the masks of self-deception slip away we have to let go of people and life situations that have been holding us back and preventing us being fully who we are. It is a scary thing to do, to step into our truth and reclaim our birthright when we have been taught our whole lives to avoid truth at all costs, to keep up the façades and not rock the boat. But the more of us who make these choices, the easier it becomes. And the more we attract into our lives people who have made the same choices and appreciate us for who we honestly are.

Rocking the boat is what we are here to do!

Isn't it exciting and exhilarating when you stand up for what you truly believe in? Our time has come, and the old ways are not working anymore. Paradigms are crumbling and new ones are rising in their place. As we understand eternal truths, we see the world for what it is, and understand how desperately things need to change.

We align with our higher purpose, the divine intelligence, and see what our life's path is. What mission have we been given? What is our role here at this time? It is to wake the world up, to guide humanity through the massive shifts and changes that are taking place. And of course, that starts with ourselves. We must awaken ourselves, and we must keep the balance between being fully awake – masters of our own reality, knowing that we create everything with our own energy, taking full responsibility for our lives as a manifestation of our own inner state of being – and being of service, helping to awaken the sleeping masses, and doing everything we can to help people through these times.

And you know what the best part is? It's fun. Believe it or not, the universe actually wants us to be happy, it doesn't want us to suffer. And the more we work with the universe, the happier we become, the less we suffer.

We are used to a duality in our minds over food. When I grew up, I had issues around my weight. I was trapped in a no-win situation. I could either eat, and feel dense, heavy, fat and sluggish, or I could not eat and feel good in my body, clear and light, but ungrounded, spaced out and weak. As most teenagers do, I worried about how I looked. I fluctuated between liking the look of my body and feeling happy about myself by not eating, or satisfying my instinctive biological need for foods but not really liking myself.

I turned to drugs to help me see my way out of this duality, to escape into an artificially induced state of oneness and bliss. The chemicals I put into my body for years didn't do me any favours physically. But they did open me up to a higher state of being, an understanding that I could experience life the way I wanted to. I understood that my life's path involved trying to find ways to recreate those highs naturally, to adopt lifestyle choices that could assist me in living in my highest truth.

I turned to raw foods and yoga, and have been working with those disciplines for nearly two decades now. I can honestly say the process has been revelatory. It has been an arduous and at times painful journey but the results just keep coming, and they keep getting better and better. Every time I am opened up to a whole new level of being in myself it blows me away.

This journey is like peeling back layers of an onion. You peel back one layer, you make improvements in your diet by adding certain foods and cutting out others, make changes in your lifestyle to move closer to having the life you really want. For a while you feel amazing, on top of the world. But then you uncover a whole other layer of issues, another set of physical, emotional and mental blocks to work through, that had been lying hidden deep within you, but are now out and exposed because you have peeled off the rubbish that had been covering them.

This process never stops: it is the path we follow as humans, and the more we are in it, the more we learn to love it, to accept it all, not to resist but to enjoy it all, the ups and the downs. The pain and the pleasure are equal gifts, two sides of the same coin.

How can foods have such a transformative effect?

Thanks to films like *What the Bleep?* and *The Secret*, and books like *Messages From Water*, people are beginning to fully grasp the concept Buddha taught us: "With our thoughts we make the world." Everything is energy, and everything is connected. Every thought we have, every action we take, affects the quantum field.

The universe is a living, breathing, intelligent mass and we are inextricably a part of it. If we focus on something long and hard, we affect the quantum field. If we tell the universe over and over, "I haven't got a boyfriend, I haven't got a boyfriend," what's the result? No boyfriend. If we replace that with, "I am attracting a beautiful loving nurturing relationship into my life," result? Result.

The skill is in maintaining that focus and intent when the spanner gets thrown into the works, when we have to deal with the stuff we manifested for ourselves without realising. Every single food in this book gives us a boost to such a degree that we feel noticeably better about ourselves. When we feel better about ourselves we take more forthright action, make clearer decisions. Challenges are more easily overcome, obstacles more easily dissolved.

That's Raw Magic in a nutshell: it's a win-win-win situation. Your body, your health, your mind, your life, your family, your friends, your planet: everyone's happier. It's a simple concept, but it really does have the power to change the world.

And it's not *if*, it's *when*.

Not "is it possible?" but "yes, it's going to happen!" – once enough of us decide for ourselves that this is the future, and the future is now.

Why eat raw foods?

At the time of writing, I am in my fifteenth year of raw foodness. Every year it gets better. For sure, there are challenges: I uncover emotional issues I need to work on; I encounter situations in my life that I need to change to move forward; more problems occur that demand a clear sharp focus to resolve; physical detoxification and healing comes up. But month on month I find myself with increased levels of vitality. The joy I feel just through existing on this beautiful planet bubbles up and up; the energy and enthusiasm I have for life surges through my veins. The positivity and passion I feel for making the world a better place just keeps growing, no matter the setbacks I encounter on the way.

I am more able to keep a clear intention and understand the steps I must take to reach my chosen goals. Every time I reach a new level of awareness and under-standing, another one opens up before me. This journey is infinite, and it just keeps getting more magical.

I see raw foods as an integral part of optimum health and vitality. When you are eating pure plant foods with all their energy and life-force intact you are assisting your body in tuning into its own wisdom, aligned with that of the earth from which the plants have grown.

One of the basic tenets of raw foods is to eat food as close to the source as possible, sunfoods. So we don't generally eat animals and animal products, because the animals have gained their nourishment from the plants, and the plants are one step closer to receiving energy direct from the sun. Many superfoods, such as maca and gojis, grow in mountainous regions – they are literally closer to the sun! Raw foods assist us in helping our bodies vibrate at the highest possible frequency; eating this way unlocks the potential within us to become more fully who we are.

Raw foods form the basis of a successful health programme for a variety of reasons.

Enzymes   When we heat food above 38 °C (118 °F) the enzyme content is destroyed. Enzymes are necessary for almost every function in the body, especially digestion. As children, our bodies manufacture all the enzymes we need, but after adolescence we stop being able to make them ourselves and become dependent on food sources to get them. Enzymes are associated with ageing; a diet high in enzymes promotes youthfulness and immortality! I consider them so important, I take extra enzyme supplementation with my raw food diet, which I find gives me even more energy and immunity.

Nutritional content   Nearly all foods have a higher nutritional content when eaten raw: heat destroys many vitamins, minerals, and amino acids. There are a few exceptions, such as lycopene, found in tomatoes and carrots. Lycopene can still be absorbed by the body if the cell walls have been broken down, by juicing for example. In addition, watermelon has more instantly bioavailable lycopene than tomatoes, so we really don't need to cook our food to get lycopene.

Whole, unprocessed   Generally, raw fooders eat foods that are less denatured. They are consuming less chemicals and artificial additives and preservatives with their foods. They are getting more fibre, and a higher water content.

Alkalinity   Thanks largely to the work of Dr Robert Young, the public are becoming more widely aware of the benefits of a high alkaline diet. Most junk foods and heavily processed foods are acidic, causing a stress on the body that increases weight gain and decreases immunity. The ideal diet should be made up of at least 70 per cent alkaline foods. A raw food diet high in vegetables easily satisfies this requirement. When our systems are alkalized, we feel calmer, can think more clearly, feel more on top of things, and have a stronger immune system.

Immune system   Cooked foods put a greater strain on the immune system than raw foods. When cooked foods are eaten the body has an immune response known as leucocytosis. This does not occur when raw foods are eaten, although cooked foods can be eaten if they form less than 50 per cent of the meal and the raw foods are eaten first, in which case the body does not produce leucocytes. Generally, raw fooders find they are less prone to catching viruses than when they ate cooked foods, and when they do catch them they tend to get them less severely and to shake them off faster.

Raw fooders generally eat from four main food groups: vegetables, fruits, sprouts (grains and pulses), and nuts and seeds. From these foods we can get all the requirements that conventional nutritionists state we need.

To be successful, I believe a raw food diet should consist of at least 50 per cent vegetables, the majority being green vegetables such as lettuce, spinach, rocket, broccoli, kale, celery and cucumber. The green leafy vegetables contain the most minerals and are also a surprisingly good source of protein. Juicing vegetables is an excellent way to up our daily intake.

Fruit should be eaten minimally as a high fruit diet upsets blood sugar levels and can contribute to tooth decay. Try to eat local and seasonal fruit in preference to tropical fruits, which have lost a lot of their freshness and vitality as they have been shipped across the world. The best fruits to eat are berries because of their dense nutritional make-up and they are our ancestral foods.

Nuts are a good source of protein but are generally acidic and mucus-forming. Soak nuts before using to activate enzyme inhibitors, and try to use seeds in preference. Seeds such as sesame, sunflower and pumpkin are highly nutritious, more easily digestible, and less acidic.

Sprouted foods like lentil, alfalfa, sunflower, wheat and buckwheat are one of the best sources of nutrition because they are guaranteed fresh, raw, seasonal and locally grown! Sprouts have a super-high nutritional content and are cheap and easy to grow yourself.

My current thinking is that the ideal daily raw food diet should look something like this:

- Two to three litres of the highest quality water available
- EFAs in the form of flax oil and hemp oil, at least 1 tablespoon
- Vegetable juice, at least half a pint
- One or two main meals made with organic seasonal vegetables, soaked nuts and seeds, with sprouts
- Sea vegetables, at least ten per cent of total daily food intake
- Superfoods, at least ten per cent of total daily food intake
- Minimal fruit and dehydrated snacks, no more than twenty per cent of total daily food intake

I believe for raw foods to become successfully integrated into our existing lifestyle, it is important not to get too fixated on our diets. Many people fail because they set themselves too high goals which they can't stick to, and then they feel that the raw food diet must not be for them. For it to be sustainable it is far better to introduce raw foods gradually than rush at it headlong. Just increasing 50 per cent of your diet to raw will reveal the benefits to you, especially when combined with daily consumption of superfoods. The rest will come in time.

Raw is a journey not a destination; it is the key to a door but we must walk through the doorway unassisted, with no crutches. When being 100 per cent raw becomes the goal, we are missing the point; if sticking to the diet is making us unhappy because we can't share food with friends, we are getting it wrong.

Emotional health is just as important as physical health, and it is vital we keep that perspective: preparing and eating your food with love is just as beneficial as the quality of the food itself. When done properly we shouldn't have to think about it; raw is there to enable us to live our lives more fully, to free up energy to enjoy ourselves, not to become another set of rules to be entrapped by.

Raw foods open up a whole new paradigm within us, a world of unlimited life and abundance, where there is no death just a continual rebirthing process. The potential for the transformation of humanity as more and more people open themselves up to this way of being is mind-blowing.

If you are interested in finding out more about raw food nutrition and want some recipes to get you started, I go into more detail in my earlier books, *Eat Smart, Eat Raw* (Grub Street, 2002) and *Raw Living* (Grub Street, 2007). I also highly recommend the books of David Wolfe and Gabriel Cousens, two raw food pioneers working in the USA. If you are only going to buy one raw food book, I would suggest *The Sunfood Diet Success System* by David Wolfe.

What are superfoods?

I adore superfoods. I have been eating them every day for over two decades, and I can say unequivocally that they provide me with that edge which helps me deal with the demands of life as a woman in the 21st century. Of course, I could do fine without them, but I don't want to just do fine, I don't want to just get by: I want to live a fulfilling and abundant life, and superfoods are a major factor in my being able to juggle and balance the varying and often contradictory elements of my world.

I run a successful business, I enjoy many creative projects, I spend large amounts of quality time with my three children, I have a full and fun social life, and I get plenty of time in solitude to meditate and reflect. I am not leading a life that anyone is incapable of, and I don't come from an exceptional background. I have had little support from family and society in my life because of the unconventional paths I have chosen to take, and I have lived for long periods of my life in relative poverty.

But I had a dream, and I kept focused on that dream, and my focus has led me to this point today. As a teenager growing up in the 1980s I knew there must be more to life than the picture of doom and gloom presented to us in the media and the drudgery and boredom of my parents' lives. I sought to find alternatives, to find a deeper truth, a more beautiful way of living. My journey brought me back time and time again to the answer that all we have, all we need, is here in the moment, and the more we live life in our highest truth at every turn, the more we are rewarded.

"Being the change" means being aligned in body and heart, constantly reminding ourselves of our focus and our truth in life, of how we can play our part to make the world a better place. And that is how I came to be so passionate about superfoods, foods that help create that inner and outer alignment in our lives.

"Be the Change you wish to see in the world"
– Mahatma Gandhi

People are becoming more familiar with the idea of superfoods, but there still remains a lot of confusion as to what actually qualifies as a superfood. I would classify them as natural plant foods which have two primary qualities: firstly, they are exceptionally high in nutrition and thereby provide the body with increased energy; and secondly, they have special intrinsic properties which can enhance our lives greatly. In my book, broccoli and blueberries are not superfoods! They may be excellent food choices, but they don't have the incredible charge and power of true superfoods. True superfoods really do make superbeings!

Because all the nutritional properties of these foods are so packed in, they are amazingly efficient, and make the body's job of extracting what it needs and utilising it so much easier. When our bodies are getting their requirements met abundantly, and when the digestive process isn't being strained in the process, so much energy is released that we feel the revitalizing effects very quickly. This is a major factor in their growing popularity; the difference in your performance between when you take them and when you don't is remarkably obvious. Superfoods are in a different league to supplements because they are actually whole foods. Their natural synergy is preserved and the messages they send to the body are much more easy for it to receive and process than those of isolated components that have been manufactured in a laboratory.

As you are reading this book, you are very likely wondering why you haven't heard of many of these foods before. Most of them grow in areas where the land is purer and unspoilt because the indigenous populations are living lives of isolation and poverty, still relatively untouched by Western materialism. They are often celebrated and revered in their native countries but unheard of outside of the regions where they are grown. As we Westerners start to realise the importance of really treating our bodies as temples, demand for innovative and original products increases, more research is done, and we are being introduced to many exciting new discoveries. As word spreads about their efficacy, people are joyfully consuming superfoods on a more and more regular basis. That's one of the things about these foods: they may seem expensive at first, but once you start to experience their benefits, you appreciate their value. You can't put a price on the sort of improvements superfoods can bring into your life, your priorities shift, and they become more central to the weekly budget than a few DVDs, a trip down the pub, or a weekend away.

If you are looking at the many superfood blends that are on the market, then I would advise you to remember that old adage, "You get what you pay for." There is no such thing as a bad superfood, and I have never come across one which cannot help with healing to some degree, but the quality between brands varies immensely. Some are bulked out with cheaper fillers, others are of a higher potency. But what you are paying for when you buy these products is the formula development, the complicated manufacturing process of blending the powders to an exact recipe, the packaging and the branding. When you are taking the superfoods in this book, in my experience the body responds better because it is not being overwhelmed by the complex information contained in these branded blends. The body is like a child, it works best when it's being treated in as straight-forward and uncomplicated manner as possible, and is much happier being given one or two toys at a time to play with than a huge toybox where it's just going to lose half the pieces and then not be able to find the bit that it wants!

When you first enter the world of superfoods, it can be hard trying to decide which ones are right for you. They all have unique qualities which makes it hard to say that one is better or worse; it's like trying to compare peas and carrots or an apple with a banana. Some days you fancy an apple, some days are banana days; some people always gravitate towards the peas and others are more carrot people. It's best to start with just two or three so you can notice their effects and get to know them – then you can tune in and decide which ones you need at a particular time. It's also not easy recommending a daily dosage. It is always advisable to start off with a little and work up until you reach a level you feel comfortable with. Often the body will go through a healing crisis as it rebalances. Old complaints like skin problems or gut reactions may flare up, in which case return to a minimum maintenance dose, allow yourself some time to rest and let the body do its thing, and after a few days you should be feeling you've reached a new level of vitality as you've cleared your old stuff out.

Virtually all the superfoods in this book contain substances that regulate the body's metabolism and thus control cravings. They help us tune into the body's natural appetite, so that when you are eating superfoods on a daily basis it becomes really hard to overeat or undereat. When superfoods are an integral part of your daily diet you just don't get hungry in the same way. Low blood sugar, unhealthy food cravings and issues around weight become a thing of the past. Weaknesses over food start to fade away and sustained energy and vitality replace them.

When I wrote *Eat Smart, Eat Raw*, one of my sayings was, "If you want to lose weight, stop counting calories and start counting nutrients." Perhaps now we should change that to, "Stop counting calories and start eating superfoods." Not only are weight issues a major factor in illness, they are a preoccupying concern for so many people in society, particularly women.

Think how much female power will be released when women stop obsessing over their dress size and are able to channel that trapped energy into more positive and creative pursuits!

It is the alchemy contained within these foods that puts them in the elite class of superfoods. It is an incredible nutritional profile, combined with an amazing vibration from the land where they are grown, and then presented within an easily accessible and bioavailable form that the body naturally recognises and understands. Superfoods are "you can have your cake and eat it" foods, foods of enlightenment, foods of the gods. They fulfill both our needs from food; to be delicious, nurturing, irresistibly good, and satisfying, but also to meet all our nutritional requirements and fuel our bodies to the optimum.

It's all about the love

You need to love your food while you are eating it, and it needs to love you while it's in your body. It's all about the love, and double the love isn't just love plus love, it creates a magic which is infinite love. Eating these foods causes chemical reactions in your brain that put you on the right pathways; they guide you back to yourself, your inner wisdom, and enable you to make empowered choices to create the life of your dreams. When we are living in accord with our higher intelligence we become tuned in to ourselves and each other, and the magic flows. These foods nourish our bodies at the deepest level, the cellular level, and when we create harmony and alignment in our bodies, it manifests in our lives. That's why superfoods create superbeings. And the world really needs more superbeings right now.

How to have a magic day, every day

A fulfilling and healthy lifestyle needs to contain a balance of elements to keep you running on all levels. If you are too much in your head, on the computer all day, you'll always be feeling a lack, something missing in your life, because you're stuck in one place ignoring so much of the world around you.

Likewise if you spend a lot of time doing things for other people and none on your own doing things for yourself, you're going to start feeling resentful and used. We find fulfillment through service, through giving, through knowing we have done our bit that day to make the world a better place. And we need to keep that in balance with the work we do on our own inner soul growth. Too much giving and we get burnt out; too much complacency and we are not contributing to the greater good.

It demands skill to keep the balance between fulfilling our roles in the world and preserving our internal core, a skill which in itself needs working on and developing throughout our lives. I believe we need to include five elements in our daily routines to keep whole, to keep dancing. Of course we rarely get to include them all every day, but if we make them our focus, if we keep them in balance within the week, then everything else flows around that.

1 **Exercise** is integral to a healthy body, oxygenating the blood and stimulating the lymph. Daily stretching helps to relieve tension and improve mental clarity, loosening mental as well as physical rigidity.

2 **Love** makes the world go round. Human beings need to love to flourish as much as we need food and water. Spending time with people you treasure and who treasure you is the most important part of your day.

3 **Service** What is your gift? Your unique individual special talent that no-one else has? What do you love to do to make other people happy? This is your life's work, your mission on the planet, and is usually manifold.

4 **Food** of love is the biggest gift we can give ourselves. Feed yourself the best organic, seasonal, local produce available, and see the world offer you the best right back at you.

5 **Meditation** Time spent alone is essential for inner peace. Even if you can only find ten minutes early in the morning, that is time well spent to set your focus and intent for the day.

I have friends who are healers, singers and mothers; artists, musicians and fathers; managers, writers and chefs. Many combine something in the healing arts with something creatively expressive; many combine something more left brain like teaching with something more right brain like design; the vast majority do not have a "boss" but work independently. In virtually every case, what we do benefits those around us *at the same time as* enriching our own lives.

As we come into our power we discover these different strands to ourselves, and it becomes our passion to share these with the world. This is what we mean by multi-dimensional beings: people who are experiencing life in all its different facets, who enjoy a rich and rewarding social life, family life, love life, work life and creative life, and who successfully dance between the different, often paradoxical aspects of themselves by retaining a deep connection to their divinity.

The key to a happy life is simplicity and sustainability. If we are all living in tune with the environment and in harmony with our fellow beings, if we are not plundering the earth's resources and abusing her abundance, then our needs can be met effortlessly. All the most effective tools for living are simple, easy and often free.

As we come together with the same vision we develop communities that operate harmoniously and make life even easier as we share the burdens and responsibilities of day-to-day life. We live in simple and sustainable dwellings, and we grow our food simply and sustainably; we spend our time in pursuits that give back to the earth rather than benefiting man at the earth's expense; we use natural household and bodycare products, and clothes, bedding and towels made of fabrics like hemp and organic cotton.

We don't need endless possessions because we have inner peace, we don't consume more than is necessary because we have inner contentment. We don't pollute the water and the land with chemicals. This is the paradise vision: it is easy to achieve and simple to manifest, once it becomes the consensus reality. Playing in Gaia's garden, nurturing and being nurtured, healing the planet with our love, one day at a time, one acre at a time. It's not an impossible dream – there are communities already living this way, and the more of us who move towards this vision the more possible it becomes.

When we are flowing with the universe, the universe looks after us. When we are living in our most spiritual truth, vibrating at our highest level, magic occurs and miracles manifest. Our needs are met, we are provided for, our dreams start to come true. Synchronicities abound, joy overflows, love is everywhere. All it takes is that leap of imagination, to step out of the box, to take risks with the unknown, to not be scared of not understanding and not being in control. It just means taking small steps every day, moment by moment, and before you know it, you have the best life ever.

How to get your B12

This is one of the most common questions I get asked. Where do you get your B12 from? Do you take supplements? There are many rational answers I can give to that question, facts and statistics I can trot out. I have looked into the subject, and it is not something I worry about. If you want to know more, I would refer you to the work of Gabriel Cousens who is very knowledgeable on the subject and whose opinion I respect greatly.

What does concern me, and what I believe is more valuable to share with you, is how to get your cosmic B12. Twelve ways to find your Bliss.

1   **Everything happens for a reason.**   There is a divine intelligence at work in the universe that is orchestrating a whole grand masterplan. We cannot expect to comprehend its workings, that's why it's a higher intelligence. When we hand over that control and understand we are just actors on a stage, that brings with it a huge sense of relief and inner peace. The more that you hand the power over, the more the universe looks after you, and the more you can just enjoy being in the moment.

2   **I am doing exactly what the universe wants me to do right here and now.**   Find the perfection in the moment: it is always present, it's just that we cannot always see it. But know that you are right where you are meant to be, doing what you are meant to be doing, at every instant.

3   **My job is to be a clear channel for my higher self to work through.**   All we need to do is access the divine intelligence that exists in each and every one of us, encoded in our cells, our DNA. We also hold programming, patterns both inherited and learned, which blocks the messages of our DNA. So it is a perpetual dance between working on clearing the channels, and manifesting the intentions of our higher selves.

4   **All that matters is the moment.**   The whole of reality exists right in the here and now. It always was and it always will be. All that matters is being in the moment and accessing the divine within it. If you think what you're doing in the 3D is important, or that you understand, or that you're in control, you're on the wrong track. Truth is a magical mystery beyond our present state of understanding.

5   **Love it all.**   Everything that happens to me is a manifestation of my own holographic matrix; outer reality is simply a reflection of my own inner state of

being. So all I see is a part of me, and the best way to deal with anything that troubles us is to love it into submission. Love dissolves all patterns.

6   **It's all an illusion.**   The material world is an illusion, a thinly disguised veil for multi-dimensional reality. It's a game, and it's our mission to see through the veil, penetrate the illusion, and reveal the hidden truths within the matrix.

7   **Money and time are tools created by the dark forces to enslave us.** Money is not real, it's the biggest illusion of them all and everyone buys into it. The universe is abundant, and if we are serving her then she will take care of us. Time is only a linear representation of a point in an infinite universe and as such is a pretty meaningless way of plotting change and growth. Being always present in the moment you enter the bliss of the eternal now.

8   **All darkness comes from a sense of separation.**   There is no separation only oneness: separation is illusion, we are never alone. Find the unity and the oneness and dissolve the darkness, the fear, anger, resentment and lack.

9   **There are beings from other dimensions looking out for us.**   We are far from being the only intelligent life force in the universe. Angels, archangels, ascended masters, members of the Galactic Federation, they are all around us, guiding us, nurturing us, loving us.

10   **Humanity is going through a shift in consciousness.**   We are at the dawn of a new golden age – ascension, enlightenment, there are many different ways to look at it, all of them inadequate for the full multi-dimensional glory that we are just beginning to get glimpses of.

11   **We find fulfillment in service.**   The more we walk our truth and help guide humanity into the light, the more fulfilling a life we lead. The more we give, the more bliss we receive. Balance that with your own inner work to find perfection in your life.

12   **The universe loves me and it wants me to be happy.**   Whenever you feel troubled and challenged, just repeat this mantra. It's not going to be hard this time, it's going to be easy. The universe loves me and it wants me to be happy.

The left brain/right brain dichotomy

It was Tony Wright, a long-term UK raw foodist, who introduced me to the mind-shatteringly brilliant concept of left and right brain functionality. He did not invent the theory by any means, but he has devoted himself to exploring the relationship between the two hemispheres of the brain, particularly in regards to raw foods.

It is scientifically established that the two hemispheres of the brain have different functions.

The left hemisphere is responsible for tasks we think of as more male-orientated: linear, rational, logical thought. The left-brain is the I, the independent thinker, the ego, which understands itself as separate from the rest of the world, an isolated part. This is where our competitive instinct comes from, as we feel we must fight for self-preservation; it is also where we feel fear and anger.

The right brain is the more feminine aspect of the mind; the creative, nurturing, giving aspect. The right brain has no sense of self, ego or separation, it experiences the self only as part of the greater whole, in oneness and union. The right brain has no understanding of time, it occupies the infinite moment. The right brain is the genius inside all of us, a unique spark of creativity that has something unrivalled and extraordinary to offer to the world.

Western culture is left-brain dominant. Some of us may have developed our right hemispheres more than others, but all of us are ruled by the left brain, the notions of time and the fight for self-preservation being controlling factors in our lives. Tony's theory is that it was not always like this; that what is Biblically known as the fall was the point when man left paradise and became left-brain dominant. In order to achieve enlightenment, to recover our natural state of bliss and return earth to the paradise garden it once was, we must learn to balance the two hemispheres.

It is a startlingly simple concept, and one into which all paradigms fall. It doesn't matter which religion, which psychoanalytical theory, which social or scientific model you look at, they all fit into this one simple paradigm. All the ills in the world can be whittled down to one cause: the repression of the right brain by the left.

Raw foods stimulate the right brain; superfoods fire up the right brain, especially cacao. Meditation, yoga, chanting, and all creative and artistic pursuits, all help build new pathways in the brain which create a greater state of balance. As we move more into our right brains, we literally learn new ways of thinking. We begin to consider what is good for the whole in a given situation, not what will purely benefit ourselves. We operate less from a place of fear, poverty and scarcity, and more from a place of love, trust and abundance. Because we are tuning into the universal mind or infinite being, synchronicities abound – and time and again things miraculously fall into place at the last moment. We are in the flow, and the flow is strong in us.

In my experience, eating superfoods is the surest and easiest way to build up the right brain and create new pathways. Cacao is the major way to do this, especially in combination with other superfoods containing rare trace minerals like Etherium gold and Blue Manna. The longer we consume these foods on a daily basis, the more we open up to our inner worlds (the right brain) and are less constrained by society's expectations of us, our left-brain programming.

Here's a simple table to give you some examples of the right brain/left brain dichotomy. These are just a few, light-hearted examples. Like the right brain, the possibilities are endless...

Left brain	Right brain
stagnation	growth
the city	the sea
alcohol	Ayahausca
chasing	magnetism
chatter	silence
lies	truth
imposed order	natural order
domination	resistance
repression	ascension
being a victim of circumstance	creating our own reality
lower self	higher self
driving a car	riding a bike
agony	ecstasy
CAPITAL LETTERS	lower case
pain	bliss
schools	home education
holding on	letting go
contraction	expansion
confusion	clarity
time	eternity
constipation	big fat poos
restricted	free
dissatisfaction	gratitude
overeating	fasting
destruction	creation
being asleep	being awake
hell	heaven

Cacao

The cacao bean comes from the cacao fruit, which is a pod growing mainly in Africa and South America, similar to a papaya. Consumed by the native people, the fruit is delicious, white and creamy and not overly sweet; similar to custard apple. Each fruit contains between 20-50 beans, and the cacao bean is what all chocolate is made from.

Denatured chocolate bars

Why have we only recently discovered the health benefits of chocolate?

The average bar of chocolate you find on the newsagent's shelves is made from cocoa solids. Cocoa solids are made by taking the beans, fermenting them, then drying them out. The beans are then cleaned and roasted, and this heating process destroys many of their nutritional properties. The roasted beans then have their shells removed and the result are the nibs, broken up bits of bean. The nibs are then intensely heated again, so the oils melt to form what is known as chocolate liquor. The chocolatiers take the cocoa solids and at very high temperatures, mix them with ingredients – usually milk, sugar and emulsifiers – to make a chocolate bar.

So the cacao bean goes through three heating processes, has many of its beneficial oils removed, is combined with foods that are not optimally healthy, and the chocolate that we experience is but a poor shadow of the real thing.

EU regulations state that to be called milk chocolate, a bar must contain at least 14 per cent cocoa solids – so in a high street chocolate bar, only one seventh of the actual ingredients have to be this denatured form of chocolate, and the rest is fattening, bad for your teeth, acidic, and unbalancing for the blood sugar! It is similar to having only been fed white sliced bread our whole lives and suddenly discovering the power of the whole wheat grain; or only drinking orange juice made from concentrate out of a carton and having freshly squeezed for the first time.

Despite this, it is still one of the most popular foods on the planet. There is no other food which people become so openly and willingly addicted to! This gives us some idea of the power of cacao.

"I could give up chocolate, but I'm not a quitter." - *Anonymous*

History

Pottery evidence of the use of cacao dates back to Honduras in 2000 BC, although the human use of cacao fruit may go back as far as 15,000 years. It originates from South America, and the first civilization considered to have cultivated cacao was the Olmecs of Mexico.

The Mayans learnt about cacao from the Olmecs and made it a central part of their civilization. There is much archaeological evidence of pottery and wall carvings, some of their rulers were named after cacao, and they even had cacao gods. As well as imbibing cacao, they used it in coming of age rituals and as a sacred offering in religious ceremonies.

The Aztec civilization followed that of the Mayans, and they too conferred great prestige on the cacao pod. The beans were so revered by the Mayans and Aztecs that they used them as currency. In the Aztec city of Texcoco, the city budget was as much as 32,000 beans a day! One fish was worth three cacao beans, one avocado was worth one cacao bean, a canoe was one hundred beans. Incredibly, they continued to be used as currency in Mexico until 1887.

It was the Spanish explorer Hernan Cortes who conquered Mexico in the sixteenth century and brought cacao to Europe. Cortes described cacao as, "the divine drink which builds up resistance and fights fatigue. A cup of this precious drink permits a man to walk for a whole day without food." Christopher Columbus also recorded coming across it on his travels.

Carl von Linnaeus, the 18th century Swedish scientist, gave the tree its Latin name, *Theobroma Cacao*: "cacao, the food of the gods". Now, over two-thirds of the world's cacao is grown in Africa, mainly on the Cote d'Ivoire.

Nutrient-dense

In its raw, untampered-with state, the cacao bean is one of the most nutrient-dense foods known to man. It contains over 300 chemical compounds, making it one of the most complex and nutritionally significant foods available to us. It is a premium source of minerals, vitamins, antioxidants, protein and healthy fats.

"Anything is good, if it's covered in chocolate."
– Jo Brand, comedienne

Minerals   Cacao is one of the very best known dietary sources of magnesium and sulphur. Magnesium is an essential mineral which most of us are deficient in. Like calcium it is important for building strong bones, and assists in converting EFAs in the body. It provides essential support for the heart, helps relieve PMT and is a natural laxative. It is an excellent source of sulphur, known as the beauty mineral because it is so beneficial for the hair, eyes, skin and teeth. Cacao also contains significant amounts of iron, phosphorous, and the B vitamin group.

Antioxidants   Cacao contains 10 per cent antioxidant flavonols, nearly twice the amount found in red wine and three times that which is found in green tea. The antioxidants in cacao are easily absorbable by the body and have been shown to assist in cardiovascular health and help prevent against cancer. The ORAC score is the official US measurement for antioxidant levels in food. The ORAC score for raw cacao powder is virtually off the scale – 995 units per gram, at least seven times more than that of normal dark chocolate.

Neurotransmitters   Chemicals which transmit nerve impulses across a synapse, i.e. they effect chemical reactions in the brain. Cacao is home to the neurotransmitter anandamide, known as "the bliss chemical", an endogenous cannabinoid naturally found in the human brain. Cacao is the only food other than cannabis to contain cannabinoids. Cacao also contains anandamide inhibitors, which means that our bodies' abilities to break down anandamide is decreased and so the blissed-out feeling lasts longer. Cacao also contains significant amounts of tryptophan, an essential amino acid which the brain uses to make the neurotransmitter serotonin. Serotonin is known for the feelings of euphoria it creates; the dance-drug Ecstasy causes large amounts of serotonin to be released in the brain.

Phenylethylamine   PEA is known as "the molecule of joy", and only present in two foods: chocolate and blue-green algae. It is the chemical produced in the brain when we are fully happy and immersed in the moment, especially when involved in a creative act like writing or painting, dancing or listening to music. PEA is also very good for the brain and improves brain function. When I take the PEA extract blue manna I feel more focused, alert and intelligent. Physically it promotes healthy joints and tissues. And if all that wasn't enough, PEA also affects the neurotransmitters dopamine and norepinephrine, which increase mental positivity. It is the presence of PEA that largely seems to account for the common folklore wisdom that chocolate makes a good substitution for sex, as we get the same increased levels of PEA when we are in love. "Some 50 per cent of women reportedly claim to prefer chocolate to sex, though this response may depend on the attributes of the interviewer." (www.chocolate.org)

Aphrodisiacs   A box of chocolates is the most popular gift to give on Valentine's day. As well as the loved-up feelings we get from the PEA in chocolate, the neurotransmitters affected by chocolate make us feel happy and alert, and the minerals magnesium and sulphur both loosen the muscles and make us more relaxed. On top of that, cacao is one of the best dietary sources of arginine, an amino acid also known as nature's Viagra. Arginine increases blood-flow to the heart and the genitals, increasing arousal and improving sexual appetite.

MAO inhibitors   Cacao contains monoamine oxidase inhibitors (MAOIs) which inhibit monoamine oxidase enzymes (MAOs). This has the effect of increasing the levels of neurotransmitters in the body, and having an anti-depressant effect. When we are young we naturally produce high levels of neurotransmitters, thus MAOIs facilitate a youthful attitude to life and have anti-ageing properties. They also act as an appetite suppressant. Cacao seems to have the effect of regulating the body's natural appetite: it helps us tune into what our bodies actually need, rather than eating out of habit or for emotional comfort. Most regular consumers of raw cacao report weight loss and an improved ability to stabilize their weight at the level they feel most comfortable with. Additionally, MAOIs are present in significant amounts in shamanistic plants such as ayahuasca. This would account for the enhanced psychic sensibility that many cacao-lovers experience.

Stimulants   Cacao contains subtle amounts of the methylxanthines caffeine and theobromine. These are both stimulants; however, both are proving to have far different effects when consumed raw rather than cooked. The presence of caffeine is one of the primary reasons people cite for avoiding chocolate, but in our experience the caffeine in raw chocolate has little to no effect. Personally, I have a highly developed and sensitive system which cannot tolerate even small doses of toxic substances such as alcohol and caffeine. Before we discovered raw chocolate, if I were to eat even the tiniest amount of cooked vegan dark chocolate I would feel the negative effects of the caffeine. I get a tense, wired, edgy feeling from caffeine that I never get from raw cacao. When we first started making chocolate bars one batch of cacao nibs we were sent had been toasted by accident. It only took a few days of consuming these toasted nibs for us all to notice an increase in aggressive feelings and mood swings. This to me was enough proof that the caffeine in cacao only has negative effects once it has been heated. Homeopathic research has come to a similar conclusion, that the physiological changes are caused by substances released during heating.

Why is cacao such a magical food?

Why do people go completely crazy for cacao, while others are vehemently against it? I believe cacao is a wake-up food. It wakes you up to your full power, to who you truly are, to the potentiality of the moment, to the infinite and abundant nature of the universe. For a lot of people this is too much to handle. We are brought up to believe in limitation and suffering. For people whose whole lives are based around this paradigm, cacao brings up too much fear. How could I step outside of the box I've created for myself? How could I let go of my ego's definition of who I am, and be fully, spiritually in the moment? For many people this is too big a leap to make, and they cannot find a place for the cacao gods in their hearts.

But for the majority of people the opposite is true. Most people feel limited and restricted in their lives. They are dying to break out of the box, to live a bit more freely, to embrace who they fully are and be given a chance to soar. Cacao gives them a taste of what this could be like and that is a wonderful feeling. And remember: with our thoughts we create the world. When we experience that cacao high, every time we break out of a restricting thought pattern, we are telling the universe we are willing to accept a greater truth, a higher reality.

For example, you are having a tough morning with the kids. Two of them are fighting and the baby has had you awake all night. There is a big pile of washing to do, and a heap of emails you are dying to get a peek at. It's 11 am and you are starting to flag. Eat a piece of toast, or a few rice cakes, and you are more likely to stay locked in that negative pattern. "How hard this all is; why do mums get so dumped on; why don't I have more help?"

But eat some raw cacao with its super-dynamic loved-up switched-on energy, and your whole mindset changes. You find yourself laughing at their bickering instead of taking it seriously, and rather than shouting at them and losing your temper, you join in the rough and tumble and make a game of it. Or you notice what a glorious sunny day it is outside and bundle them all up to the swings where you bump into one of your favourite friends and sit there putting the world to rights while the children get to burn off their energy. The vibration you are sending out to the universe then is that parenting is fun and easy, and miraculously the universe sends you situations that match that vibration; your husband comes home and spontaneously attacks the wash basket for you instead of watching TV, and a friend offers to have the kids over the next day which gives you a chance to disappear into your emails. Whereas if you had been in a grump all day about the hopelessness of your situation and the misery of parenthood, that is just the situation the universe delivers for you, the next day, and the next day, and the next day, until you can change that record in your head.

Cacao is the food of the goddess

Goddess energy is about being in the moment: it is about surrender, acceptance, and loving everything. It is about flowing, and being present and giving, giving, and more giving. When we eat cacao it puts us right back in touch with our goddess energy. It puts us fully in the moment, and loving it, ready to give some more.

For instance, you have had a long busy day at work. You've come straight home for dinner and had a delicious raw soup. You know you should call your mum because she called over the weekend and you haven't had a chance to return her call; she will be waiting, getting anxious that you are neglecting her. Have some ice cream for pudding and you'll more likely end up in front of the TV, feeling guilty that you haven't called again. But eat a piece of chocolate as an after-dinner treat, and bam! There is that extra energy you needed to pick up the phone and show your mum you really do care. You speak for half an hour, and she feels so much better because she got to speak with you, and you feel so much better because you made your mum happy.

Cacao is also a major sunfood. Sunfoods are the foods that carry strong yang energy: they are expansive, they help us reach up and out and are strengthening and energising. They keep our energy rising and ascending. Thus they help us deal with our blockages, because they give us the insight to rise above them, to meet them head on and to move beyond them.

Perhaps there is a boy that you like. He said he would call that evening, but he has a habit of letting you down. When he does call, he is always charming and funny and gorgeous; unfortunately, he more often doesn't call than he does. Instead of sitting at home wasting time on MySpace, waiting for the phone to ring, you eat some raw chocolate, call up a girlfriend, and go out for a dance. And who knows, maybe you meet a charming, funny, gorgeous boy who does call!

Are you getting the picture now? At first sight it may seem simplistic to say that a food can change your life. But what we are really saying is that your consciousness creates your reality: with your thoughts you make the world. Basically put, we are all a chain of chemical reactions, endless cause and effect. The food you put in your mouth is made of many chemicals; these have an effect on your body and consciousness; which then has an effect on how you react to any given situation; which then has a knock-on effect on the rest of your day, your week, your life, and also the lives of everyone you come into contact with.

Cacao has over 300 chemical constituents – it is one of the most complex foods known to man. It melts at body temperature, so when you put it in your mouth all those chemicals explode as they hit the tongue. So it is such an all-encompassing, expansive, abundant food that that is how you feel when you eat it; it gives you the ability to feel that you could deal with any situation that arises in the next moment; it makes you feel god-like, a superbeing. This is what we mean when we talk about superbeings: people who are so in their flow, so in tune with their higher purpose, so aligned with their inner truth, that they are not afraid of living in their full power; they know they can deal with whatever life throws at them. And precisely because they are so positive, so visionary, so fearless, they attract fewer and fewer situations of stress, doubt, negativity and poverty, and instead create a reality about them that is blissful, assured and abundant. I think the best thing about being a superbeing is the other superbeings you get to meet.

Another magical property of cacao is the way it acts as a platform for other foods. It has a synergistic effect on the ingredients that you mix it with that increases their effect exponentially. For that reason I often put a little cacao in with my other superfoods. You don't need a lot, just half a teaspoon of powder or a teaspoon of nibs, but it gives them a lift, an extra edge. Instead of just taking maca straight, mix a little chocolate in and the effects will be maca to the power of maca, maca squared. It's like cacao raises the vibration of whatever it comes into contact with; it shines a spotlight on it and allows it be fully who it is, it brings out the very best qualities of a food. Naturally, this works in reverse as well: a tablespoon of maca or a teaspoon of suma in your chocolate rounds out the cacao experience, brings an extra depth to the cacao magic, enhances the alchemy.

Balancing opposing forces

Many religions teach that the road to enlightenment is through a balance of the opposing forces within us. Life as we know it is about duality, and what propels us on is the search for a resolution within that dynamic, a striving to find the unity, bliss and oneness behind it all. It is a perpetual dance between yin and yang, the dark and the light, heaven and earth. The more we learn to combine those energies, to allow them to co-exist within us, the closer we get to reaching nirvana. Cacao is the food of enlightenment because it is a sunfood (yang) and it is also the food of the goddess (yin). It brings together the two polarities within us. How does it do this? Culturally, we are taught to think of foods as either good for us and boring, or bad for us and fun; "you can't have your cake and eat it."

When I was a child, eaters were divided into two clear-cut categories: the sanctimonious, weird and dull people who ate brown rice and lentils, or the life-affirming brigade who embraced everything and drank, smoked and ate dead animals. Gradually over the decades those stereotypes started to dissolve as the do-gooders realised they had to acknowledge their dark side, they couldn't abstain for ever unless they really did want to be miserable; and the omnivores started to get sick in ever-increasing numbers.

Cacao dissolves all those stereotypes completely. Here is the richest, darkest, most delicious, decadent, luxurious, divine-tasting food ever, and it also happens to be one of the number one dietary sources of minerals and anti-oxidants on the planet. One slice of one of my chocolate cakes has more nutrition in it than what most people would consider a healthy meal, something like stir-fry and noodles. When eaten on a regular basis, cacao really does blow your mind, because it blasts all your preconceptions of what is good and bad out of the window. It allows you to live beyond duality, to dance in the one. You can discover your darkness and live in your light all at the same time. It is the mother and the father energy all rolled into one; it nurtures you and comforts you, then it kicks you out the door and tells you to get the hell on with it.

What else? Yes, there's more, there's always more. Because cacao is the food of abundance. It helps us to experience the universe as infinite and eternal; it opens us up to the sense that we can keep flowing, keep living, keep loving. Life stops being a series of deaths and rebirths, and turns into a continual ecstatic, "Yes!"

www.naked-chocolate.com
http://www.bbc.co.uk/science/hottopics/chocolate/

Gojis

2007 was the year of the goji berry in the UK. It became the latest fad trend, mentioned in the same breath as a list of skinny A-list celebrities, flying off the shelves of Fresh & Wild, the subject of BBC News articles. So is there anything behind the hype? Are goji berries just overpriced raisins?

The Chinese have been eating gojis for over 2,000 years and are mildly amused at our sudden "discovery" of what is to them an everyday food. The Chinese consume gojis in many forms: they add them to rice and meat when cooking, they make them into wine, and they are a popular tea. In the West they are more commonly consumed as a snack, either on their own or in bars and trail mixes, or in the form of juice (although most products marketed as goji juice actually have a very low goji content).

So great is the popularity of gojis, and their contribution to the economy, that in Ningxia they hold an annual goji berry festival.

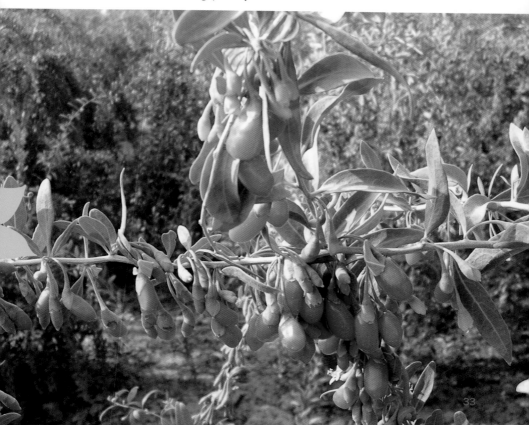

Like tomatoes, peppers and potatoes, gojis are a member of the nightshade family. I often substitute them for dried tomatoes in savoury recipes – they have a similar intense, vivid flavour.

There is some confusion as to the difference between goji berries and wolfberries. This has largely been created by one company who claim that only berries grown in Tibet can be classed as gojis, and that all the berries from China should be called wolfberries. In their marketing literature and on their website they state that Tibetan berries are superior to the Chinese ones. However, there are so few berries grown in Tibet, it seems it would be impossible to sell them commercially, and that this is just a marketing technique playing on Tibet's positive image.

Wolfberry is actually the colloquial name given to the berries by Chinese farmers, who saw the wolves feasting on them straight off the bushes. The berries grow on shrubs, and those that grow in the Chinese Ningxia region are said to be very high quality. Here they grow along the floodplains of the Yellow River, renowned for its mineral-rich silt. This is likely to be why goji berries are said to contain monatomic trace elements and be high in ormus energy (see p72): they are grown in ancient, mineral-rich soil.

The berries must be harvested carefully, and cannot be touched because that will cause them to oxidise and turn black. They are picked by hand by shaking them off the bushes and onto mats where they are sun-dried or taken to factories for dehydrating.

Gojis in the West

It was Archibald Campbell, the third Duke of Argyll, who brought gojis to the UK in the early eighteenth century – and they still flourish today in our hedgerows. Lycium barbarum is the Latin name for gojis, which now apparently grow wild in some parts of England.

Today gojis can easily be found in Chinese herbalists as well as health food shops, although the quality is variable. Generally, the more bright orange in colour gojis are the more likely they are to have been sprayed with high levels of pesticides – the deeper red, the better.

Admittedly there is some hype around goji berries in the West. In their dried form they do not contain 500 times the vitamin C of oranges. Although they contain anti-oxidants which are known to prevent ageing, it is unlikely that there are Chinese people who lived to be over 200 years old by eating them. Just altering your diet to include some goji berries will not make you lose weight, although as part of a healthy diet they will fulfill your nutritional requirements and help you tune into your body's natural appetite. But like all the superfoods in this book they have a strong nutritional profile which assists the body in many different ways. And they also have that magical energetic quality, a "je ne sais quoi" which makes them uniquely irresistible. The Chinese say the only side-effect of eating goji berries is laughing too much!

I believe their popularity is largely down to the "have your cake and eat it" factor. Like cacao, gojis are fun. They taste like yummy little sweets and you want to eat them – there is no element of chore or duty involved. But at the same time you are feeding your body one of the most nutrient dense fruits on the planet, and giving yourself high doses of many vitamins, minerals and amino acids that you might be lacking.

Benefits

In TCM (Traditional Chinese Medicine) goji berries are a yin food. They assist the liver and kidneys, enhance the immune system, and improve eyesight. Like ginseng they are a tonic fruit, and nourish the heart and the internal organs. They are a valuable protein source, containing 18 of the 22 amino acids and including all eight essential amino acids, which makes them a great food for vegans, vegetarians, and developing children.

They contain 22 minerals and trace minerals, thanks to the quality of the soil they are grown in. They are one of the best plant sources of iron and selenium, as well as containing significant amounts of calcium, potassium, and zinc.

Gojis are rich in vitamins, particularly the B group of vitamins, and exceptionally high in beta-carotene – more than carrots or apricots. It is the presence of carotenoids which gives them their reputation for improving eyesight.

They are widely recognised for the amounts of polysaccharides they contain, which boost the immune system and reduce the risk of cancer. It is this combination of carotenoids and polysaccharides which make them such a valuable source of antioxidants. Contained in the seeds of the berries are significant amounts of omega 3 and omega 6 oils, the essential fatty acids.

Goji berries are associated with love because of their bright red colour and the positive effect they have on the libido. Like cacao they are a heart-centred food, so adding a few of them to any meal can help carry the qualities of all the other foods into our hearts.

I wouldn't say goji berries are particularly energising in the same way that maca or pollen are, for instance. But they do provide us with a certain vitality, a ray of energy that no other foods provide. Because they are grown in one of the purest places on earth (the Himalayan mountains and surrounding areas) they have a pure, high vibration that uplifts us, which is why they are known as the "happy berry". It is this combination of being uplifting energetically and nourishing physically that makes them such a potent food.

This humble little berry has the ability to simply add a little sunshine into your day (which is probably why they've caught on so much in the UK!).

Maca

If I was running the country I would put maca on the NHS for everyone. Only it wouldn't be the National Health Service, it would be the Nation of Happy Superfooders. Maca is an adaptogen, so it assists the body in restoring balance; whatever your health problem, whatever stresses you are under, maca will support your body in correcting any imbalances. It has also been demonstrated to regulate hormones, so is particularly beneficial for women. In my own personal experience I have never met anyone who has not felt an improvement with maca. And unlike taking a supplement like iron drinks, or calcium tablets, where you are not really sure if you are noticing the benefits, everyone feels maca instantly. Almost immediately, users report increased energy levels and improved stamina.

Maca is a root vegetable from the same family of cruciferous vegetables as broccoli and cauliflower. It looks a little like a very large radish and is used in food preparation in the same way as other starchy root vegetables such as parsnips and potatoes; boiled and mashed, baked or fried. It is native to Peru, where it grows high in the Andes mountains.

The story of maca

Maca has a fascinating history. In 1989 it was declared one of the "lost crops of the Incas," and the plant was in danger of extinction. But over the past couple of decades interest in this amazing crop has grown in America, Europe and Japan, primarily for its effects on the libido but also as a natural alternative to steroids for athletes and a natural alternative to HRT for women.

In 1979 there were only 25 cultivated hectares of maca in Peru; now there are over 2,000. This is a very good thing for the native people of Peru, whose communities are benefiting from job creation, increased cash flow, and recognition for their culture; not just from the growth in the maca industry, but other native crops such as lucuma, yacon, and cacao. On the whole these crops are being traded fairly, with respect for the indigenous population.

Peru is one of the poorest countries in the world and their land is notoriously inhospitable. The Peruvian government are very protective of their native species and will not allow the seeds to be exported, so that they can maintain the monopoly on their precious assets. That is why you never see whole maca root (or yacon or lucuma) outside of South America; only the powders or extracts are allowed to be shipped out.

Maca has been popular among the indigenous peoples of Peru for as long as five thousand years. The Incans valued it so highly they only permitted its use in the royal courts. When the Spanish conquistadors came to Peru in the sixteenth century they came close to leaving, worn down by the harsh living conditions and their declining fertility levels. It was the discovery of maca that enabled them to stay in Peru, and they would trade in maca in preference to gold. Like cacao, maca has strong associates with gold energy, the ray that lifts us up to the sun, creates inner fire, auric expansion, and vibrational ascension.

Usage

Maca is one of the most powerful of the superfoods, so consequently you have to be very careful with it initially and use it with respect. It can have strong rebalancing and detoxifying effects. For instance, say you suffer badly from PMT every month. For your first cycle of taking maca, your PMT is likely to be more severe than ever. But by the second cycle, it should start to balance out, and by the third or fourth cycle it will be disappearing completely.

Or perhaps you suffer from Chronic Fatigue Syndrome. After a few days of taking maca you might start to feel more tired and wiped out than ever. But stick with it, and within a week those symptoms will pass, your energy levels will start to rebuild, and gradually you will recover a sustained energy and drive.

I always advise people to start off with half a teaspoon of maca. If after three or four days that doesn't seem a lot, and you aren't noticing any effects, or conversely if it tastes wonderful to you and you are craving more, then up the dose to a teaspoon. Keep upping it by half a teaspoon every three or four days until you reach your threshold. By this I mean the point at which you feel you have as much energy as you can cope with, and your detox symptoms start to reveal themselves. At this point you might want to lower the dose again, although it is important not to stop taking it completely if you want its magic to work. Once your detox has passed and you have flushed out the imbalances you can take as much maca as you like. Remember, it is just a vegetable. I take up to four tablespoons a day.

In Peru they eat it like we eat potatoes: they fry it and serve it as chips with chilli sauce at roadside stalls, or they mash it and make a kind of porridge with it. They also enjoy it as an alchoholic beverage, making beers, liqueurs, and cocktails with it.

Maca grows at the highest altitudes in the world – 9,000 to 11,000 feet above sea level. There is no other plant that grows in such inhospitable terrain. For this reason it gives us that energy to climb that mountain: if life seems like an uphill struggle to you, if you can't see how you can reach your goals, the peak of your personal mountain, maca will provide you with that inner fire and insight to keep on going.

The maca plant has a very high frost tolerance; so it gives you the strength to battle against the cold. I am known amongst my friends for having little sensitivity to the cold, and refusing to put the central heating on in winter! I am sure this is due in part to the large amounts of maca in my diet as well as the long time I have been raw. It's not that I don't notice the cold, it's just that it doesn't bother me, it doesn't disturb my internal balance. In fact, maca grows under a variety of extreme conditions: frost, intensive sunlight and high winds. Hence it gives us that really sturdy, invincible energy.

Benefits

Truly, maca provides one of the best sources of energy I have ever come across. It is instant and long-lasting. It makes me feel strong and grounded, calm and in control, not wild and over-excited like too much chocolate can! Pollen is a brilliant source of energy too, but it is high in sugar and too much can affect blood glucose levels. Because maca is a root vegetable, the energy it provides is much steadier.

It is a natural partner to cacao, and also goes very well with oats, which provide the same sort of slow-release, sustained boost. It mixes well with coconut in sweets to provide a very clear, wholesome treat. It is not unpleasant tasting, and has been compared to Horlicks and butterscotch because it has a kind of malty flavour. Not quite sweet, but not bitter either, it combines equally well in sweet and savoury dishes. Maca powder starts to react once it is mixed with water, so if you are putting maca in your recipes be sure to eat them within a few days or they get a strange, sickly aftertaste.

Like aloe vera and suma, maca is an adaptogen. This is a term coined by scientists in the 1930s to describe a plant which has a non-specific reaction in the body and no harmful side-effects. Adaptogens provide the body with "adaptation energy" and enable it to resist whatever stresses it is under and pressures it is suffering from. Thus adaptogens assist the body in maintaining homeostasis, a state of inner balance and core strength. This is why when you read about these plants, it sounds like they are good for everything. Aloe vera is reputed to help with immune system disorders like lupus and HIV, gut imbalances like colitis, Crohn's disease and IBS, skin conditions eczema and psoriasis, respiratory problems, joint inflammations, as well as being anti-ageing and immune–boosting. Directly, it is not treating any of these ailments. But indirectly, it goes to where the body needs it, it gives strength to the body and promotes self-healing. That is why adaptogens are so powerful: they are getting to the very root cause of the symptoms, not trying to treat the outward signs of disease, but enabling the body to rebalance and dissolve the patterns that are creating the disease. They are dealing with cause rather than effect. Once health challenges are dealt with in this way they are much less likely to recur than when only the outward manifestations of bad health are addressed and the inner roots left untouched.

Nutritionally, maca is a brilliant source of the B vitamin group including the elusive B12. The B vitamins are depleted in the body by stress; taking a food high in B vitamins like maca, pollen or gojis helps the body recover more quickly from stress and keep moving forward.

The 21st century lifestyle is a very stressful one due to environmental pollution and the fast-paced lives we lead; these superfoods are so valuable in giving us that energy to keep on keeping on, to meet the demands placed on us, to rise to the challenges life presents us with. Maca is a good source of bioavailable protein, containing 11 per cent amino acids, and 18 of the 22 amino acids needed to build protein in the body. It contains 31 different minerals and trace minerals, including significant amounts of calcium, magnesium, potassium, copper, zinc, iron, phosphorous, selenium and manganese, all of which are in a readily accessible form to the body. These minerals can help protect against osteoporosis, especially in menopausal women.

The cruciferous family of vegetables are known for the glucosinates they contain, which have been demonstrated to have anti-cancer properties and inhibit tumour growth. The plant sterols in maca, like those in aloe vera, can be used as a natural and healthy alternative to steroid drugs, boosting performance for athletes and helping the body fight challenges such as eczema. It helps with chronic fatigue not only because it provides healthy balanced energy levels, but because it assists the adrenal glands and raises cortisol levels.

Maca also provides many fatty acids, including lauric acid and linoleic acid (also known as omega 3, the EFA many of us are deficient in).

As maca is a hormone balancer, it is beneficial for women at whatever time of their lives they are in: if you have been on the pill, if you have irregular periods, if you suffer with PMT, if you have exceptionally light or heavy periods, if you are pregnant or breastfeeding, if you are entering adolescence, if you are pre-menopausal, in the menopause or post-menopausal. There are very few women that don't fit into one of those categories! Rich in bioavailable calcium, it is particularly beneficial for breastfeeding mothers because it will balance your hormones, provide you with your extra calcium intake, and help you deal with all those sleepless nights. As a hormone balancer it is also known as Nature's Viagra. It improves libido in both men and women and also improves fertility. Maca and cacao together are an indisputable aphrodisiac.

Maca does not contain hormones itself, so there is no danger of overdoing it. Rather, it supports the body's endocrine system which produces the hormones. The hypothalamus is the master gland which stimulates and balances the other glands in the body and is also considered to be the brain's sex centre; the beneficial effects maca has on the hypothalamus gland are central to its adaptogenic properties and aphrodisiacal effects. Maca also contains alkaloids which have been shown to increase fertility in humans – in a study done in 2000, the sexual activity of rats fed maca increased by 400 per cent!

Children love maca. It is not unpalatable, and easily mixes into their cereal, porridge or yoghurt. It boosts their protein and calcium levels, building strength in the bones and teeth. As a hormone regulator it can help prevent toddler tantrums, which are often just a result of hormonal surges overwhelming little bodies. It makes them strong, sure and confident in their bodies. When my children first had maca, they literally started climbing the walls! Reuben discovered how to straddle the doorframe and climb it to reach the ceiling, and would show off his new-found skills to any and all visitors to our house.

Maca is so much more than the sum of its nutritional value. It is the actual energy of the plant that we are imbibing, which has such a powerful effect on us holistically. Sure it is a great source of protein, minerals, and plant sterols. But it is that adaptogenic effect, that "survival against all odds" element that it contains in its cells, that is so beneficial to us in the West at this time in history, when we are battling against so much within our culture, and trying to adapt to the new millennium unfolding before us. That's what makes maca magic!

www.macaroot.com

Pollen

Like algae, bee pollen is a perfect food, in that it contains every single known nutrient that the body needs. Theoretically, if you were stranded on a desert island, you could live on bee pollen and water alone. Pollen is also like algae in that it is a primordial food, one of the oldest foods on this planet, and so it must be made of something pretty amazing to have made it this far. Probably more has been written about pollen than any other food in this book: its incredible healing and rejuvenative properties are well-researched and documented. Like all the superfoods, it is the synergistic effect of so many important nutrients that makes pollen so powerful, but it also contains substances as yet unidentified by science which add to its unique magic.

Bee pollen is actually a bit of a misnomer because pollen does not come from bees, it comes from flowers, and is collected by the bees and brought back to the hives. Strictly speaking, pollen is not a vegan food, but I personally feel it is unlikely that Mother Nature would have designed the perfect food for humans and not meant us to eat it.

Pollen is a great superfood because it tastes so nice, sweet and rich like honey. Children love it, it is a wonderful food to add to their diets and increase their nutritional intake. It is easy to sprinkle on cereal for breakfast or add to trail mixes and desserts. Pollen has a

> "If the bee disappeared off the surface of the globe, then man would only have four years left to live." – *Albert Einstein*

very "buzzy" energy; it is sometimes called natural speed. I remember the first time I took it, it was about 10.00 at night, I had just put two children to bed, I was home on my own, and didn't know how I was going to face the rest of the evening's chores, tidying the kitchen and sorting out the washing. I took two pollen tablets to get me through those last few hours, and ended up with enough energy afterwards to dance around the living room!

Pollen is a great food if you are always on the go, flitting from one activity to the next like a bee flying from flower to flower. If you are eating a meal that is a quick stop gap, with no time to rest or think, then adding pollen to it gives you that boost to rush off, full of enthusiasm and energy, rather than dragging yourself on feeling tired and reluctant.

The quality of bee pollen can be quite variable and depends a lot on where it is gathered from. Ideally, the environment in which the flowers and bees are living should be as pristine as possible, which is why desert pollen is very good. At one of the world's largest pollen producers they drive around the land in electric cars to minimize pollution.

As a fresh food, pollen goes rancid easily. If it is kept in packaging which exposes it to the light for long periods of time the quality can deteriorate. It also doesn't like being exposed to the heat so is best kept refrigerated. You can tell if it is past its best by putting pollen granules in a glass of water – if it floats, it's rancid. The majority of pollen that is sold in the UK is dried – if you can find fresh pollen it's really in a class of its own. Look out for the French Percie du Sert pollen which is sold frozen to preserve it. Pollen also goes off quickly when it is ground up, so if you are adding it to recipes, better to use it in its whole form unless you are planning on eating it straight away.

Most commercially available pollen is pollifloral, i.e. it comes from more than one variety of flower. Monofloral pollen is made when the bees collect pollen from one type of flower only, linden or hawthorn for example. Monofloral pollens have quite distinct tastes, and act on specific physical and energetic areas according to the flowers that they are from. For example, linden pollen is calming for the nerves, hawthorn nourishes the heart. The most beneficial pollen is that which is sourced locally to you, because then it is helping your body to tune into its immediate environment.

Pollen is produced by the flowers and collected by the bees, who bind it with enzymes and carry it back to the hive in their pollen sacs. These sacs are then brushed off the bees' legs with a fine brush as they enter the hive, and collected by the beekeepers. Bees seek out the most nutritious pollen, so flowers compete for bees' attention as a means of ensuring their survival. In order to achieve reproductive success, flowers try to produce the most nutrient-dense pollen possible, which ensures that pollen is always of the highest possible quality.

Interestingly, when scientists have tried to replicate pollen in laboratories, by taking all pollen's known constituents and mixing them together, they have been unable. Bees in the hive live on pollen, but bees fed on this replicated pollen die. This proves that pollen contains some unidentifiable substances that must contribute to its special potency.

"Bee pollen works, and it works perfectly. Pollen allows super-stars to increase their strength and stamina up to 25 per cent. This increase in strength and endurance may be the key to the secret regenerative power of bee pollen. The whole beauty of bee pollen is that it's as natural as you can get." – Alex Woodly, director of Education Athletic Club, Philadelphia, USA

Pollen can help with allergies and hayfever; if taken at least six weeks before the hayfever season starts, symptoms should be very much reduced. This works in a similar way to homeopathy: minute doses of the substance the body is allergic to builds up resistance so that when the body is exposed to larger doses, an immune response has been cultivated and no symptoms occur.

The airborne pollen that people have a problem with is known as anemophile pollen grains; the kind that is collected by the bees is the entomophile pollen grains. Pollen has been shown in studies to have the same immune-strengthening results with other allergic reactions such as asthma and sinusitis.

Because it is rich in enzymes, people often find pollen gives them digestive discomfort when they first take it because it is so stimulating to the gut. If this is the case, it is best to take it alone rather than with other foods, and consider a course of enemas or colonics because it is likely that old matter in the gut is being stirred up.

Many people also find they are allergic to pollen. Out of all the foods in this book, pollen is the one people are most likely to have a problem with; people commonly report itchy skin or tingly lips. This is due in part to the fact that we all have weakened immune systems due to antibiotic use, pollution in the environment, poor diets and not enough exposure to nature. If this is the case, you can either fast to cleanse the system before trying pollen again, or just build up slowly. If you keep taking minute amounts of pollen daily, your resistance will build up and you can gradually increase the dose until your immune system is restored and the pollen doesn't have the same detoxifying effect.

Bee pollen's use goes way back into history: it is recommended in the Bible, as well as by Pliny, Pythagorus and Hippocrates. It is also mentioned in ancient Chinese and Egyptian texts.

In Russia, where pollen has been much researched, inhabitants of the villages near the Caucasus mountains are renowned for their longevity, with many centenarians living amongst them. In the 1970s some American scientists investigated their extraordinary longevity and found that there were many bee keepers among them, and the common factor was the "scrap honey" they all ate — the residue from the bottom of the hive, rich in pollen, propolis and other beneficial substances. Like royal jelly, another popular therapeutic bee product, pollen is well regarded for its anti-ageing properties, as it stimulates cell renewal and so rejuvenates the skin.

Pollen contains at least 96 nutritional elements. It contains all twenty-two amino acids, consisting of 40 per cent protein, weight for weight more than any animal product.

Bee pollen is a great dietary source of B vitamins. Whenever we get stressed our B vitamin levels get depleted, so taking pollen is an excellent antidote to stress. If we have had a stressful incident in our day, for instance getting stuck in a traffic jam and then not having enough time to get ready for an important meeting, or having an argument with someone and then having to take the children out somewhere, taking some pollen gives us the energy to carry on without feeling depleted. It is one of the best dietary sources of vitamin B6, and a reputed source of the hard-to-find B12.

It is a good source of vitamin C, the best dietary source of rutin, a glucoside which strengthens the capillary system, and one of the richest sources of carotenoids and bioflavonoids. Pollen is a great source of minerals, especially zinc. It has significant amounts of potassium, calcium, phosphorous, magnesium, silicon, manganese, sulphur, selenium and iron.

Benefits

Here are some more of the benefits of pollen:

- As far back as 1948, research was published that showed that taking bee pollen acts as a prevention against cancer and can reduce tumours. It has also been demonstrated to protect against radiation and help with the side effects of chemotherapy.
- Pollen is good for fertility; it is literally the sperm of the flower, the male seed produced in large quantities to ensure some of it succeeds in carrying on the species. It stimulates the ovaries and improves the libido. Due in addition to its high zinc content, it is particularly good for prostrate problems.
- It is favoured by athletes for its abilities to increase stamina and endurance, and was used by Muhammed Ali to "float like a butterfly, sting like a bee." There are many, many reports from sportspeople and sports trainers who have used bee pollen to improve their performance.
- It is rich in lecithin, which helps to metabolise fats in the body. Lecithin contains substantial amounts of phosphatidyl choline, which is beneficial for the brain, especially for children whose brains are still developing. For this reason also, it is a great food for pregnant women. Bee pollen has great synergy with flax oil, because the lecithin in the pollen helps ensure flax oil's abundant supply of EFAs are broken down and absorbed properly.
- It is a great source of the nucleic acids RNA and DNA, the building blocks of the body.
- Like coconut oil, it normalizes cholesterol levels in the blood and balances the metabolism, so helping with weight loss.
- Like algae, it is a superb source of phenylananine, which regulates the body's natural appetite.

- It rehabilitates the gut, strengthens the intestines, and has been used to treat Crohn's disease, colitis, and digestive ulcers.
- It is a natural antibiotic.
- It is popular for pets, for boosting their immune systems, improving the quality of their coats, increasing longevity and as an aid to fertility.
- It has been used to treat anaemia, it boosts the circulation, aids cardiovascular health, regulates the blood sugar, and has been extremely successful at treating a huge variety of weaknesses and illnesses.

Pollen and cacao together is a brilliant source of positive energy. When you eat pollen and cacao, you feel like you can do anything! As pollen has a natural sweet-ness, it complements the bitterness of the cacao well. We often make trail mix just by mixing up some pollen granules and nibs up with a few other snack foods like goji berries, coconut chips, or yacon root.

http://www.shirleys-wellness-cafe.com/
http://alternativescentral.com/beepollen.htm

The algaes

There are three types of nutritionally dense algae commonly consumed in the UK: spirulina, Klamath Lake blue-green algae and chlorella. My personal preference is for Klamath Lake algae because it is a wild food, and I believe it is important to consume as many wild foods as we can on a daily basis. Wild foods provide us with a direct connection to the earth, their natural state hasn't been tampered with, they are more whole, and so have a stronger vitality.

Spirulina and chlorella are both farmed algaes. However, spirulina is considerably cheaper, and more suitable for eating in large amounts. So if you're going for bulk then spirulina would be a better choice. I would rarely eat more than 1 tsp of Klamath Lake algae at a time, whereas I often eat several tablespoons of spirulina in a guacamole or a smoothie. Chlorella is not so readily available as spirulina and Klamath Lake algae, and is most often found in tablet form.

The algaes are one of the most nutrient dense foods known to man, and the highest vegetable source of vitamin B12. The controversy rages still on B12 analogues and algaes. Latest research suggests that chlorella contains usable B12 but spirulina contains B12 analogues which block the uptake of true B12.

Algae is a purely natural plant food, which goes through minimal processing to reach us in edible form. Algae was the initial life form on earth, and blue-green algae dates back over four billion years. There is evidence to show that algae was one of man's first foods: races such as the Aztecs and Incas harvested and ate raw algae. Tribes in Africa still depend on it for their sustenance, and it has been used in Chinese medicine throughout the centuries.

When we eat algae, we are connecting with a profound and ancient energy.

Richard France, a macrobiotic counsellor, states, "It is not inconceivable that on subtle vibrational levels, unique genetic memories and messages of harmony and peace are stored in algae, which have grown undisturbed for years in a pristine environment. This information may be passed to us at a cellular level, encouraging harmony among our own cellular family."

> "Spirulina can help restore our lives. It's the next best thing to eating sunlight! Eat algae and bring light into your own cells. Consume less and live lighter on the Earth. Magnified by millions of people, life begins to change. This is a magnificent legacy for our next generations."
> – Robert Henrikson, founder of the world's largest spirulina farm

Not only do the algaes contain a high density of vitamins and minerals, as well as many other health-giving properties, it has an assimilation rate of over 90 per cent – which means that all these nutrients are readily absorbed and used by the body.

With many supplements formulated in laboratories, the nutrients are not in a form that can be utilised by the body, and so go to waste. Many work with each other; for instance, the body needs adequate levels of vitamin C to absorb iron, so when iron supplements are taken on their own they are ineffective if the correct levels of vitamin C are not present in the diet. However, in blue-green algae we find the ideal balance of nutrients for our needs.

Nutritional profile

If you were going to design the perfect food for humans, with every single nutrient present in optimum ratios, it would have a remarkably similar nutritional profile to these algaes.

The algaes contain:

- All the essential trace minerals: boron, calcium, chromium, cobalt, copper, iron, magnesium, manganese, phosphorous, potassium, sodium, zinc and vanadium, in perfect balance for optimum health.
- Vitamins thiamin (B1), riboflavin (B2), pyrodoxine (B6), niacin (B3), vitamin B12 (see above), vitamin C, choline, pantothenic acid (B5), biotin, folic acid, and vitamin E, also in exactly the right balance for maximum bioavailability.

- All eight amino acids, and in a form more easily digested by the body than those found in meat and vegetable protein (85 per cent assimilable, whereas beef is only 20 per cent assimilable).
- Thousands of live active enzymes. Enzymes are a little-mentioned component of health, yet vital to every process of the body. They are completely destroyed by temperatures of over 118 degrees centigrade: consequently, all cooked food is devoid of enzymes, and many of us may be lacking in sufficient amounts to ensure vitality, especially in winter months when our intake of fruit and salads tends to be lower. A daily dose of blue-green algae can be invaluable in providing us with some of this precious resource.
- The highest source of chlorophyll in the plant kingdom, as well as other health-giving pigments. Chlorophyll is an amazing healer and helps to correct over-acidity in the body. I provide more information on chlorophyll in the section on wheatgrass. The presence of chlorophyll is one of the elements which makes algae such a great detoxification food. Taking algaes has been shown to assist in removing heavy metals from the body. In 1993, studies showed it had beneficial effects on children from Chernobyl suffering from radiation sickness.
- RNA/DNA, nucleic acids essential in the reparation of cells and growth of body tissue.
- Essential fatty acids. These fats are vital to good health, but as they are only found in fish, and seeds such as flax and hemp, they are often lacking in a vegan diet.
- One of the highest known natural sources of beta-carotene, a rich source of vitamin A.

The algaes can be used on a daily basis simply to sustain good health, but they have also been used to treat conditions such as IBS, Alzheimer's disease, anaemia, hypoglycemia, liver fatigue, depression and candida. They have been proven to aid concentration and memory, strengthen the immune system, and counteract over-acidity in the body. They enhance cardio-vascular health and reduce cholesterol levels, and have been used in the treatment of serious illnesses such as cancer and AIDS.

International research has been going on into Spirulina for decades, and there is much evidence to support these health claims. Unlike many health foods, where there is no funding made available for research, manufacturers who see the huge economic potential of Chlorella and Spirulina as a retail product have commissioned many in-depth, scientific papers.

Spirulina

Spirulina is a farmed algae, produced mainly in Hawaii and China. It grows at very fast rates and provides more nutrition per acre than any other crop on the planet. It can even be grown in the irrigation beds in rice fields. As such it is one of the most ecologically responsible and sustainable foods available. Under a microscope it looks like green spiraling threads, hence the name. It is a very hardy plant and can adapt and grow in many different environments; thus it provides us with that ability to adapt and thrive in adverse conditions. Spirulina contains over 60 per cent protein; per acre, that means you can grow 20 times more Spirulina than soya beans, and 200 times more than beef!

Chlorella

Chlorella is so named because of its exceptionally high chlorophyll content. It is a single-celled algae which is cultivated mainly in Asia. In Japan it is eaten by 7 million people daily and is more popular than vitamin C supplements! What singles out Chlorella from the other algaes is the Chlorella Growth Factor, or CGF. The entire reproductive cycle of Chlorella can take place in 24 hours given the right conditions. What the CGF factor exactly is, remains a bit of a mystery. But it means it is effective at cell restoration, tissue repair, and is very beneficial for growing children.

Klamath Lake blue-green algae

Klamath Lake blue-green algae is currently one of the few wild, uncultivated strains of algae growing in the world. It is harvested from the Upper Klamath Lake in Oregon, USA. The Klamath Lake basin acts as a 'nutrient trap' for the surrounding 4,000 square miles of secluded wilderness in the Cascade Mountains. Seventeen rivers and streams feed the lake with a rich supply of minerals, volcanic silt and many other nutrients. So pure are their waters that the locals refer to them as "The Rivers of Light". To get the maximum benefits from algae it is vital that it does not reach extreme temperatures during processing: heating or freezing will destroy it. Look for algae which has been flash-dried, as this leaves the cells of the algae intact and retains its bioactivity.

Klamath Lake algae is also an invaluable addition to a child's diet: as any parent knows, it can be a challenge trying to strike a balance between a child's fussy habits and meeting their nutritional needs. Algae is great for children because you need such small amounts: just a quarter of a teaspoon a day can be smuggled into their favourite foods, acting like a kind of safety net in meeting their nutritional needs, ensuring their health and your peace of mind.

Algae is also a great thing to feed your pets: it is reported to improve their coats and hair, and increase longevity.

Klamath Lake algae comes in many different forms: liquid, powdered, tablets or capsules. E3-Live is a specially freeze-dried algae which comes in liquid form to preserve its nutritional properties. My favourite form of taking it is as Crystal Manna, manufactured by an American company called Ancient Sun Nutrition.

Crystal Manna is one of the most out-of-this-world foods I have ever come across – green and sparkly, it looks just like fairy dust. If you think of Masuro Emoto's book *Messages From Water* and imagine your cells to be snowflakes, every one is a crystal

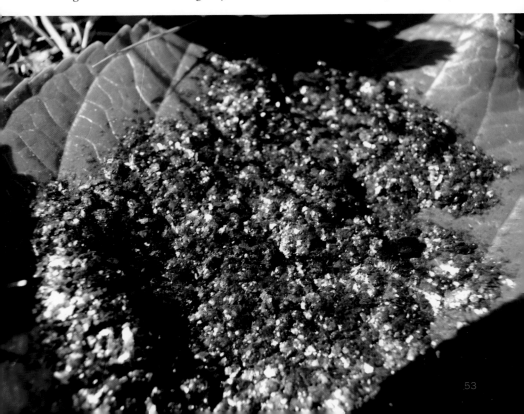

like that. Our bodies are mostly water, after all, and everything we put in our bodies is going to affect our snowflakes. If we eat food that has been mass-produced, with all the life taken out of it, that is going to damage our snowflakes — make them into crumpled and distorted patterns. But when we eat superfoods, their vital energy is so strong, they help our snowflakes become beautiful.

Crystal Manna is such a beautiful food, when I eat it I feel like my snowflakes are crystallizing into amazing patterns — literally, I feel sparkly!

Blue Manna is also produced by Ancient Sun Nutrition, and is another of my favourite foods I eat every day. Blue Manna is the blue pigment extracted from Klamath Lake algae. This extract is very rich in PEA and phycocyanin. As we discussed in the section on cacao, PEA is known as "the molecule of joy". It is naturally produced in the brain when we are in states of bliss, totally involved in an activity that we love. It makes us completely present, lost in the moment, oblivious of outside distractions.

PEA is a great brain food. It sharpens the mind and creates clear, focused intelligence. Phycocyanin is a natural anti-inflammatory and very beneficial for the joints. Taking Blue Manna every day helps us keep sharp and on the button. Because of the pathways it creates in the brain, it leads us to make choices that are following our bliss and empowering us creatively rather than ignoring the gifts and talents of our heart or feeling scared of taking decisions that inspire us. Of course algae contains PEA and phycocyanin, so just taking algae will ensure you get these elements in your diet, but Blue Manna enables you to receive them in a more concentrated form.

www.spirulina.org.uk
www.spirulina.com
www.watershed.net/chlorella

Wheatgrass and barleygrass

Wheatgrass and barleygrass are virtually identical. They are among the most alkaline foods available. As such, they are very calming, nurturing and purifying.

They are most commonly consumed freshly juiced or in powdered form. Growing your own wheatgrass and juicing it yourself is one of the most powerful cleansing techniques known in the alternative health field.

Anne Wigmore first popularised the use of wheatgrass for therapeutic purposes back in the 1930s. She tried a variety of different grasses and found wheatgrass to be the most beneficial. Along with Viktoras Kulvinskas, she founded the Hippocrates Health Institute in Boston. Now run by Brian and Maria Clements in Florida, Hippocrates is world-renowned for healing people with apparently terminal illnesses. They have countless testimonials from patients who have been given no hope by their doctors – people suffering from heart disease, cancer and diabetes. Using a living foods programme with large doses of wheatgrass as a central plank of the regime, they have nurtured thousands back to optimum health.

The use of barley, for food and nutritional purposes, dates back to ancient times. Roman gladiators ate barley for strength and stamina. In the West it was first known for the barley grain it produces.

Nutritional profile

Barleygrass contains eighteen amino acids, including eight essential ones. It also contains a variety of vitamins and minerals, including beta-carotene, folic acid, vitamins C, E and five B vitamins (including B12), calcium, iron, magnesium, and phosphorus. Barleygrass is said to have: thirty times as much vitamin B1 and 11 times the amount of calcium as cow's milk; three times as much vitamin C, six times as much carotene and nearly five times as much iron as spinach; nearly seven times the vitamin C of oranges; and four times the vitamin B1 of whole wheat flour.

Wheatgrass contains 20 per cent protein, which includes a balanced blend of twenty amino acids, and nearly double the amount of beta-carotene found in carrots. It is one of the best sources of chlorophyll available. It contains over 90 trace minerals.

Drinking 1 oz wheatgrass juice is the nutritional equivalent of eating 1 kilo of fresh vegetables! As such, it's the ultimate convenience food, a sure-fire way to get your daily requirements in. In juice form it is instantly absorbable by the cells, ensuring maximum assimilation.

"Wheatgrass juice is the nectar of rejuvenation, the plasma of youth, the blood of all life. The elements that are missing in your body's cells – especially enzymes, vitamins, hormones, and nucleic acids can be obtained through this daily green sunlight transfusion" – *Viktoras Kulvinskas, author Survival Into The 21st Century*

People sometimes worry that if they have an intolerance to wheat they will not be able to consume wheatgrass. Most people who avoid wheat do so because of the high gluten content of the grain once it has been cooked. In raw wheat grain, the starches turn to sugars when they sprout, so there is no gluten content. Unless you are celiac, a condition which means you should avoid all wheat products entirely, wheatgrass is a safe and beneficial health choice.

As well as their excellent nutritional profiles, the grasses carry first-class enzymes into the cells when they are consumed freshly harvested. They have been shown to neutralise and digest the toxins in our cells. Consequently they have antiseptic, anti-bacterial and deodorizing properties. They contain an enzyme which increases resistance to radiation, and are used on people suffering from radiation sickness.

The grasses can also be used externally due to their high antioxidant capabilities. They are great for the skin and hair, and are sometimes used as poultices. They can relieve the irritation of eczema, psiorasis and sunburn, and are used for all types of wound healing – bites, stings, cuts, sores and boils. Chewing wheatgrass or applying it to the infected area can help with toothache and freshens the breath. You can even put it in the bath!

Grow your own

Wheatgrass is so simple and easy to grow. All you need is organic wheat grain, organic compost and a seed tray with a lid. Soak half a cup (60 g or 2 oz) of wheat grain overnight and then in the morning, drain and leave to sprout for around 12 hours. When it's ready, spread a layer of compost on the seed tray, and spread the seed evenly over the top. Water, and cover with the lid. Leave it in a warm, light place for four days, by which time green shoots will be starting to show. After four days, remove the lid and water daily for another three days, by which time you should have a luscious green crop.

If you have a high-power juicer, you can push the grass straight through: one tray should make about 8 oz grass. If you have a high-power blender, put a handful in the blender jug with a glass of water and blend for a couple of minutes. Strain and serve. If you don't have either of these pieces of equipment, you can just chew the grass and spit out the fibre, which is indigestible.

By harvesting the grass before it forms a seed, you are consuming it when it's at its peak – when its nutritional level is at its highest. It is recommended to start with just a 1 oz shot of wheatgrass juice every day, and work your way up to 2 oz. Most people consider 2 oz enough!

A fantastic way to detox is to drink a shot of wheatgrass or barleygrass juice for breakfast every morning. It makes most people feel sick – this is the liver cleansing and releasing bile. If you try wheatgrass and it doesn't make you ill, don't get too cocky! It's more likely that the toxins are deeply buried and you're not absorbing the grass properly. Keep drinking it every morning and chances are, within a few days, you'll be wanting to retch!

The best way to think of wheatgrass is like medicine – it's not going to taste nice, but you know it's going to make you feel good. But I still looked forward to it because I knew once I'd got it down me, I'd feel calmer, clearer and cleaner.

The powders aren't as effective and are much more costly, but they are still a brilliant way to alkalise your diet. Barleygrass powder has quite a pleasant, sweet-edged taste, which makes it more palatable to add to recipes. If you read the ingredients lists on the labels you'll see that many of the superfood blends on the market are mainly barleygrass or wheatgrass powder, or sometimes spirulina. They are usually expensive because you are paying for the development of the blend and all the packaging and marketing. Buying pure barleygrass or wheatgrass powder is a much more economical way of getting these green superfoods in you.

You can also obtain frozen juices. Freezing destroys a little of the enzymatic content and nutritional properties, so it's not as beneficial as fresh juice, but still better than not at all. One way to take the juice is to make a whole tray of it, then put in into ice cube trays in the freezer. You can add these cubes to drinks, so you just get a flavour of grass in your drink, or defrost a couple and drink them neat.

People often raise the contradiction between recommending locally grown foods and seasonal eating, and promoting superfoods, as I do. My feeling is that ideally, we would all be eating foods picked wild from the surrounding area. But the modern day diet is so far from that point that we need some assistance getting back to the ideal. Due to unsustainable farming techniques and environmental pollution our food lacks the potency and mineral qualities that it once had. The superfoods act as a bridge: they are intense foods that help restore our nutritional balance and give us the brain fuel to make the right choices to get back to an ideal lifestyle. But wheatgrass and barleygrass are the ultimate superfoods because they fulfill both criteria.

When you grow your own grass it costs pennies and uses minimal resources. You can put your loving energy into the grass as you grow it, so you know that it's never been maltreated. When you juice it fresh it's 100 per cent alive, all the enzymatic activity is intact, and you know it's not been depleted by travelling halfway across the world.

The magic in the grasses lies in the fact that chlorophyll is the most similar substance to human blood known. It's identical but for the fact that the iron molecule present in haemoglobin is replaced by magnesium in chlorophyll. Magnesium is a mineral that most of us lack in our diets. So when you drink wheatgrass juice, which is 70 per cent chlorophyll, you are literally drinking green blood, plant blood.

You are oxygenating your blood, cleansing out all the rubbish and restoring your cells to their natural state of perfection. Chlorophyll is the basis of all plant life, it is the first product of light, so when you drink fresh juice you are effectively drinking liquid light.

When you set yourself up with such a strong cleanser first thing in the morning, it has a powerful knock-on effect on the rest of your food choices for the day. Wheatgrass balances the blood-sugar, so you're less prone to mood swings. Fewer emotional ups and downs mean you're less likely to reach for the junk food when you have a dip. A balanced blood-sugar also knocks sugar cravings on the head.

Before I started drinking wheatgrass daily, I had a passion for dates. Fresh dates were one of my favourite treats, a comfort food when I was feeling knocked-out. Dates are a good source of minerals but extremely destabilizing to blood sugar levels. As I started consuming fresh grass daily, I noticed dates start to taste over-sweet to me. Before long, I lost my craving for them completely.

If you are having problems with candida, wheatgrass is one of the best ways to kill sugar cravings and help you stick with a low-glycaemic diet. These effects also help with weight management. Once you've drunk your wheatgrass, eating is usually the last thing you feel like doing while your body processes and cleanses. And once it has done its work and rebalanced your blood, you're going to feel revitalised and far less likely to reach for the snacks. Put a clean liver, a balanced blood-sugar and an even emotional keel all together, and you've got guaranteed weight-loss. So like all the superfoods, the power of the grasses can't be measured just in their nutritional value. They have a deeper effect on our energy and consciousness that will ripple out to all areas of our daily lives.

www.hippocratesinst.org
www.greenlifefoods.co.uk
www.shirleys-wellness.cafe.com

Purple corn, camu camu and suma

These very special foods were largely unheard of in this country until recently. Like the monatomic trace elements, they are virtually a cross between vibrational essences and foods.

You only need to take them in almost homeopathic doses to feel the effects: it is as much about getting the vibration of the plant into your body as experiencing the nutritional benefits. In fact, these foods are so potent that large doses can be detrimental, having such an extreme effect on the body. The first time we had purple corn we shared one teaspoon between six of us and were amazed at the noticeable difference we felt.

Purple corn

Purple corn comes from the Amazon and is mainly grown in Peru. It is a rare strain of normal maize, different from the blue corn found in some breads and tortilla chips. In Mayan cultures it is very revered, a sacred plant, and central to their mythology.

An ancient Mayan prophecy says that when purple corn comes to the West, that will be the shift between the ages: the time of remembrance.

Purple corn is said to activate the ancient cellular memory and reconnect us with the wisdom of our DNA. Purple is the colour of the pituitary gland, the third eye, the colour of psychoactive awareness, seeing beyond the veil into the unseen world.

Many people believe that to eat holistically is to eat a rainbow diet — to include all colours of the spectrum in our diet. The colours of the lower chakras, red, orange, yellow and green, are easy; but blues, purples and pinks are often lacking. Just getting that purple ray into our diet can fill a part of us we weren't even aware we were lacking.

Purple corn is one of the best dietary sources of anthocyanin, the potent antioxidant found in blueberries. This antioxidant reduces cholesterol and is a natural anti-inflammatory. It has a fruity flavour and makes a wonderful addition to any dish, sweet or savoury, that you want to add a purple tinge to. In Peru they make a drink with it called "chicha morada."

Camu camu

Camu camu came along to steal the vitamin C crown as it contains a whopping two grams of vitamin C in every 100 grams of fruit. This may not sound like a lot compared to the amount in a high-potency vitamin C supplement, but the vitamin C in camu camu is in its natural bioavailable form. It works in synergistically in the body for maximum benefit.

Camu camu is a berry that grows on shrubs in the Amazon rainforest and looks similar to grapes. It is a powerhouse of phytochemicals including amino acids, minerals like calcium, potassium, and iron, the B group of vitamins, and beta-carotene. It can be used as an anti-depressant, to treat ADD and herpes. The high amounts of vitamin C it contains make it anti-viral, and help boost the immune system.

Although clinical studies have been done, there is very little scientific research available on camu camu, and doubtless this plant contains many exciting properties we have yet to discover.

We find camu camu energising, cleansing and refreshing. It tastes a little like lemon sherbet, and is a great way to balance out the sweetness of cakes and puddings.

Suma

Suma is a vine with an intricate root system that grows in the Amazon rainforest. It is one of the most powerful foods in this book and also one of the most difficult to describe.

In Brazil, suma is known as "Para Todo," which means "for all things." Like aloe vera and maca, suma is an adaptogen: it assists the body in restoring homeostasis and creates balance and harmony without any detrimental side effects. Adaptogens have a normalising effect on the body, and can be taken daily for long periods of time without overstimulating the system.

In our experience suma is such a potent adaptogen that it is a medicine for the soul. It shakes us right back into our central core and reminds us of ways in our lives that we are out of synch with ourselves. It shines a light on dark corners of our personalities that are neglected and hidden.

Suma contains a strong plant spirit and is practically shamanic in its effects. A quarter of a teaspoon is all that is needed to get the energy of the plant into you. Larger doses are not usually advised!

Its effect is so individualised, it is impossible to say what it will do for you. I have had reports of people taking it and having so much energy they have had to go for a run, or do some martial arts; other people take it and are knocked to the floor, feeling so dreamy and relaxed they can barely move.

If you are the sort of person who is always busy and doesn't slow down enough, then suma is likely to chill you out; if you are too chilled out already and need a bit of get up and go, suma will do that for you instead. It reminds you that that side of yourself exists, and that is a wonderful place to be too.

Like cacao, suma enhances the effects of other foods, which is why we like to add it to our chocolate and smoothies. As an adaptogen, suma works beneficially on the hormones, is great for PMT and the menopause, and acts on the libido. It contains most of the amino acids, minerals and trace minerals, including important amounts of germanium, and vitamins including the B group and vitamin E. It is thought that the high levels of germanium are one of the factors that make suma so potent: germanium oxygenates the body at the cellular level, and stimulates the immune system.

Suma contains high levels of saponins, which have been used in the prevention of cancer, and to regulate blood pressure. Known as Brazilian ginseng, it was traditionally used for strength and endurance.

Sea vegetables

Seaweeds are an essential part of my daily diet. They are calming, rebalancing, mineralising, satisfying and delicious. The earth's surface area is covered in over 70 per cent sea; if we want to connect with the earth holistically, it is important to eat seafoods on a regular basis. Think of how you feel at the seaside: uplifted, relaxed, expansive, energised, nourished. When we eat the foods of the sea, we are absorbing that energy into our bodies. I make sure the family has them at every meal. Seaweeds nourish us in ways most foods don't because they are a wild food: wild foods have all their vital force intact, they come direct from the earth; they make us feel connected and provide us with that free and untamed energy that is so lacking in our sanitised, fearful Western culture.

Traditionally an integral part of Asian diets, sea vegetables are increasing in popularity here in the West as people start to recognise their extraordinary health benefits and versatility. In Japan they have been eaten for many thousands of years. They are also popular in Ireland, Iceland, France, Spain, Australia, Canada and Hawaii; indeed, most countries which have large coastal regions.

There are thousands of varieties of sea vegetables and they are usually classified by colour — brown, red, or green. They are not technically a plant or a vegetable but belong to the algae family.

The most commonly found brand of sea vegetables in the UK is Clearspring. These are exceptionally high quality, produced using traditional Japanese artisan techniques, although most of them are heat-treated. The only varieties that are technically considered raw — not heated over 38 °C — are dulse and wakame.

You can pick up sea vegetables at bargain prices from Asian grocers, although the quality is variable and they are often roasted or fried, which might bring out the flavours but destroys some of the nutritional content. Incidentally, when you buy crispy seaweed in a Chinese shop or restaurant this isn't seaweed at all but a deep-fried cabbage!

Because they are dried and can be kept in the cupboard until you are ready to eat them, sea vegetables are such an easy food to use. Organic seaweeds are those that are guaranteed to have been harvested from unpolluted waters.

Nutritional profile

Sea vegetables are just about the most mineral-rich foods available, being a brilliant source of the B-group of vitamins and vitamin K, as well as a good protein source. Although they don't contain all the essential amino acids, they do contain them in a form which is easily assimilable by the body. Indeed, all the nutrients in seaweeds are in a colloidal, balanced form, so they are very bioavailable. As a wild food, sea vegetables are a source of that elusive vitamin B12, although there is some debate as to how absorbable the B12 is to the body.

"It may seem strange to be singing the praises of seaweed as a valuable source of minerals, then saying how it can be used to remove metals from the body. This is the paradox of a natural system, working both ways at the same time, removing imbalances, restoring things to the way they should be. Something that no modern wonder drug has ever managed to achieve." – *Sonia Surey-Gent, marine biologist*

They contain all of the trace minerals that can be lacking from land-grown foods due to soil depletion – essential minerals that we are often missing in our daily diet like selenium and chromium. They are a very low-calorific, high-fibre food, great for maintaining weight. They are a fantastic source of iodine, an important mineral more or less absent from land vegetables. Iodine is essential for the healthy functioning of the thyroid gland, which controls our metabolism, and so also assists in regulating body weight. They are also one of the best plant sources of calcium – half a cup of dulse or hijiki contains more calcium than a cup of milk, and is much more easily assimilated by the body.

Sea vegetables have been demonstrated to provide the body with certain phytonutrients that inhibit tumour growth. They are a natural anti-inflammatory agent, due to the polysaccharides they contain, and because of their high levels of magnesium and phytonutrients can help relieve PMT.

They are a perfect substitute for salt in the diet, containing healthy levels of sodium, in the right balance for the human body. The naturally occurring glutamic acids in seaweed act as a flavour enhancer to draw out and complement the natural flavours of any dish.

> "I once heard a story about a certain village somewhere in Canada's Bay of Fundy area where everyone ate dulse. After a hundred years or so they had to shoot an old fellow just to start a graveyard. The same village went from a population of just over two people to over fifteen hundred in the shortest span of years that anyone ever witnessed. The first old fellow to die there was 101 at his time of death. Some say he would still be alive today if he had not drowned on the way to the hospital to try and remove the bullets. Don't laugh. His poor grandmother mourned at the gravesite every day for years." – *www.rolandsdulse.com*

The two most popular sea vegetables among raw fooders are dulse and nori, but there are many more.

Dulse is a soft, purple seaweed. Unlike most sea vegetables, it needs no pre-soaking, just a quick rinse in fresh water to remove any stray shells and pebbles! It comes in two forms: the whole blade, or flakes, which are perfect as a salad garnish. Dulse is one of the few purple foods found in our diets. Purple is the psychoactive colour, the colour of the third eye, and we don't have enough of it in our diets. Like all the sea vegetables it is rich in minerals; dulse is full of calcium, potassium, magnesium and iron. Dulse is really good deep-fried and turned into crisps or you can make raw crisps in the dehydrator (there's a recipe in my book *Raw Living*). It adds a gorgeous richness when blended into tomato sauces. It is most commonly harvested from the Atlantic and Pacific oceans.

Nori comes either toasted or untoasted. The toasted sheets are light green and are commonly found in Asian grocers. Nori rolls are like the raw-fooder's sandwich. You can put anything and everything in them and roll them up for an instant and so-satisfying snack food. The Clearspring untoasted dark nori sheets are heated at 40 °C so are not technically raw. We also blend nori up into soups and sauces, where it acts as a thickening agent, or cut the sheets into small strips and add them to salads. You can buy nori flakes which go great as a garnish on just about anything.

Laver is the name also given to the seaweed from which nori sheets are made. Such is its popularity that nori has been a cultivated food in Japan for over 300 years. Once harvested it is washed and hung out on bamboo frames to dry in a process similar to paper-making. It is a reputed source of vitamin B12, and contains 40 per cent protein which is more than any of the other sea vegetables.

Sea spaghetti is an incredible food, really similar to tagliatelle in appearance and texture, although obviously with a fishy flavour! Many people go mad for it when they first have it. It tastes like it is so good you could live on it, and contains some nutrients that the body finds hard to get elsewhere. (There are some foods that when you eat them taste unique: avocados are one, the Peruvian fruit lucuma is another. When you eat them you think *I am getting something here that I know I am usually missing*, and if you don't have them for a few days you start to crave them.) Sea spaghetti is a great source of the minerals iron, calcium, magnesium, phosphorous and iodine, as well as all the essential amino acids. It needs soaking for at least thirty minutes before eating.

Wakame is a leafy green seaweed that can be added to salads or used to thicken sauces. It is a particularly good source of magnesium. We eat a lot of the Clearspring Japanese Sea Salad which contains wakame, agar, and a red algae called aka tsuno-mata. It is a beautiful mix of colours, and is simple to prepare and very tasty. It needs soaking for ten minutes before eating.

Arame has a mild, sweet taste. It has delicate, thin black fronds, similar to spaghetti. It is richest in iron and calcium. It needs soaking for ten minutes before eating.

Hijiki is a black sea vegetable, similar to arame in appearance but with thicker strands. It increases in volume to around four times its original size when soaked. It is one of the stronger tasting seaweeds, with an intense nutty flavour. It does not come to us raw, but is steamed or boiled and then dried after harvesting. However, I believe sea vegetables are such an important part of our diet, it is better to eat them this way than not at all. It needs soaking for at least twenty minutes before eating.

Kelp is a variety of kombu, usually sold in granular form. You can buy it as tablets, but we buy it loose and sprinkle it over our salads. It is the number one dietary source of iodine – 8 g kelp contains 100 per cent of the iodine RDA – so you only need a tiny bit every day. You won't notice the taste of just a quarter of a teaspoon on your food, but it's going to really boost your mineral intake. It's little things like this that make all the difference to maintaining a good health regime and not sliding off the rails. Because of its high iodine content kelp stimulates the thyroid, and is good for people who have an underactive thyroid condition. It is rich in iron, potassium, calcium and magnesium. The phytochemicals in kelp have been demonstrated to absorb radioactivity and heavy metals and remove them from the body. For this reason they are a great detox food, and especially beneficial if you are having mercury fillings removed. Kombu can be bought in whole strips and makes a great addition to cooking, although it is too tough to eat raw.

Wrack is sold in the UK under the Seagreens brand. Wrack has a complete nutritional profile – like wild blue-green algae and bee pollen it contains every single identifiable nutrient that the body requires, and probably some we haven't identified too! Like kelp it is excellent for removing heavy metals and toxins from the body, as it contains the polysaccharide fucoidan. It has been used to treat children with autism, who often have a mineral imbalance. Seagreens comes as granules, and is absolutely delicious sprinkled over salads or as a garnish for soups.

www.seagreens.com
www.seaveg.com

Monatomic trace elements

The monatomic trace elements are a group of supplements found naturally occurring in volcanic soil in the vicinity of Mount Shasta, California. They are known as Etherium Gold, Etherium Pink, Etherium Black and Etherium Red. The same company also produces a powder called Aulterra, which comes from an ancient seabed. The manufacturers describe them as "Supplements for the Spirit", and they work on a very subtle level: kind of like a cross between trace mineral supplements and flower essences.

They are vibrational remedies, restoring a lost balance within our very cells, our DNA. They contain substances that in ancient times would have been naturally occurring in the soil, but because of agricultural practices and intensive farming we have lost these links to the earth. They have a powerful transformative effect on the user, enabling deep healing and shifts in stagnant energy.

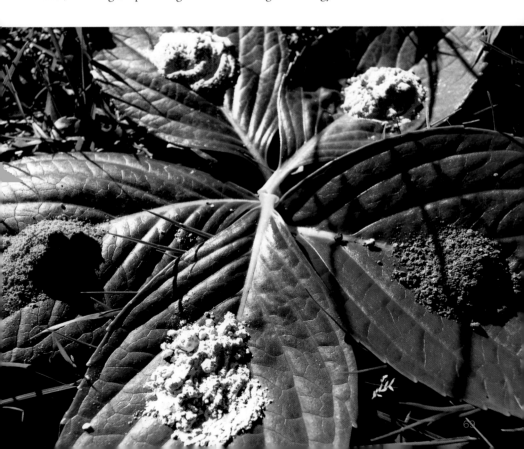

We have found them to be particularly powerful mixed in raw chocolate, where the essence of the supplement is carried right into the heart and mind in conjunction with the powerful healing vibration of cacao. This synergy seems to amplify and ground the effects, drawing it even deeper into the cells and heightening the experience.

Mount Shasta

Mount Shasta is home to many spiritual communities. There have been many sightings of extra-terrestrials and lightbeings there, and it is known for its other-worldly beauty and cloud formations. There are 28 conditions for the favourable building of a Buddhist monastery, and Mount Shasta is the only place in the world that fulfils every single one of them.

The Etheriums were discovered in a meteorite crater in the vicinity of Mount Shasta. The meteorite was thought to have landed 5,000 years ago. So you could say these substances have literally been sent from outer space to assist humanity in our transformation at this time. The Etheriums are the name given to the different strata in the soil deposits: Etherium gold is the centre of the crater, and then working outwards in rings are Etherium red, Etherium pink and Etherium black.

Harmonic Innerprizes, the distributors of the Etheriums, also produce other products such as Shamir and Chamae rose. Shamir is about remembrance; similar to purple corn it reconnects us with the ancient cellular memory and the wisdom of our DNA. Chamae rose is a shrub which grows on the Eastern side of the Sierra mountains and assists in healing and detoxification.

Usage and benefits

The recommended dose for all these supplements is only one eighth of a teaspoon, once or twice a day. Personally, as my body is so fine-tuned and I am very sensitive, I notice the effects of a single dose of any of the monatomic trace elements instantly. I find they have a profound effect on my experience of the world, and I take them every day. However, because they work on a very subtle level, many people who take them don't notice any difference at first. This is not to say that they aren't working, just that they are not noticing. I believe for people that have very deep-rooted issues, whose true self is very buried, they would still be having an effect on a subtle level which may take months to show up on the physical level.

I would recommend taking one supplement at a time to begin with. Etherium gold is the best one to start with; if you are taking one eighth of a teaspoon a day, a bottle will last you nearly two months. I take Etherium Gold every day; I usually take at least one other in a day, according to what I feel intuitively guided towards. If I want to make a very special cake or chocolate, I will put them all in: this makes for an exceptionally magical day!

Etherium gold has been scientifically proven to balance the two hemispheres of the brain. Humans spend too much time in our left brains, and not enough in our right brains; this imbalance is one of the major causative factors of discontent in our lives and in our societies. The left brain is concerned with the individual, the ego, survivalism and linear, rational thinking. The right-brain areas deal with community, oneness, bliss and creative thinking. The left brain is limited and constricting; the right brain is infinite, expansive and abundant. So many problems in our cultures are down to excessive left brain thinking, rather than thinking "outside the box", and seeing from the perspective that benefits the whole, the greater picture, rather than just the isolated self. Etherium gold assists in correcting this imbalance, in restoring whole brain thinking, "joining up the dots".

Etherium gold contains traces of the minerals gold, iridium, chromium, silver, rhodium and platinum. It causes the body to produce more alpha brain waves. These are the ones which make us feel focused and creative. It reduces the levels of beta and theta brain waves, which are the ones we create when we are stressed. For this reason, taking Etherium gold is like instant meditation.

Users report greater levels of serenity and enhanced mental clarity when taking Etherium gold; literally, it is helping us to achieve a higher state of consciousness. It helps with any sort of intellectual work: the three main foods that helped me write this book were cacao, Blue Manna and Etherium gold. Cacao gave me the heart-centred energy to keep on with it every day; Blue Manna provided me with a sharp, clear, focused intelligence, and Etherium gold kept me calm and creative.

Two independent studies, one by the Alpha Learning Institute in Switzerland in 2003, the other by the Mind Spa in the US in 1998, tested the brain waves using EEG (electroencephalogram) readings. In the Mind Spa study, the brainwave frequencies of 90 per cent of respondents balanced out. "According to the Alpha Learning Institute, this level of focus and serenity in the brain is typically only observed in people who have either spent years practicing meditation or a martial art, engaged in months of light sound therapy, or taken seminars to train the brain for maximum performance. Yet, it was accomplished in just three days with Etherium Gold."

Etherium gold is also said to assist with the manifestation of spirit into matter. Because of its electromagnetic pattern, the transformational process of energy into matter is accentuated, and the vibrational difference between thought and manifestation is reduced. This is why users report an increase in synchronicities and telepathic incidences once they start taking Etherium gold – one of the most commonly reported side-effects is an increased ability to find parking spaces! We gain mastery of our minds, and our ability grows to create the world around us as a true reflection of our hearts, rather than the distorted mirror of the ego.

Etherium red integrates the thinking and feeling processes. It assists with clear decision making, where we feel torn between our mind and emotions or have to weigh up many different factors. By integrating the head and heart, stress is relieved and clarity is created. Etherium red is also reputed to release the kundalini energy. Etherium pink opens the heart chakra. It can help release issues of sorrow, grief and past hurt. It can be beneficial for people who are too much in their heads, and puts them back into balance. When I take Etherium pink, I feel as if I am in love with everyone! Etherium black is about releasing blockages, it makes us feel grounded. It is an adaptogen, restoring homeostasis in the body and rebalancing the body's electromagnetic field.

Ormus energy

There is currently growing international interest in the concept of ormus. In the 1970s, David Hudson, a gold miner in Arizona, coined the term ORMEs – Orbitally Rearranged Monatomic Elements – when he discovered these strange materials on his land. Simply put, ormus is precious metals such as gold, rhodium, iridium, silver and mercury molecularly arranged in a different state. It has been credited with having amazing healing properties and creating profound spiritual awakenings.

Ormus is the elusive alchemical substance written about through history, in all different cultures. It is the holy grail, the Philosopher's Stone, the Elixir of Life; and taking it provides instant enlightenment. In the Bible, it is called manna, the Egyptians ate the Bread of the Presence of God, and the alchemical process of turning powder into gold features frequently in Hindu religious texts. The writer

Sir Laurence Gardner links it with the Ark of the Covenant, and believes Moses made white powder into gold on Mount Sinai.

Many of the superfoods are said to be rich in Ormus energy – goji berries, bee pollen, algae, maca, medicinal mushrooms, noni. As a monatomic trace mineral, Etherium gold has obvious links with ormus, and understanding these helps shed light on some of Etherium gold's amazing properties.

Aulterra

Aulterra rebalances and harmonises the body's energy fields. It is a naturally occurring deposit taken from ancient sea beds, high in monatomic elements, which has been scientifically proven to activate and restore DNA. New age thinking has it that rather than just the two strands of DNA, we have twelve. It is the ten hidden strands that contain encoded within them messages about our evolution, a higher consciousness. As we activate our DNA, we reconnect with the ancient wisdom of lost cultures, and also move forward into our divine consciousness.

This is ascension, and it is what many of us believe humanity is going through now at the beginning of the 21st century. Many people feel the changes in themselves, their bodies, their minds, their lives, but they do not know how to conceptualise that and they do not understand how to integrate these different experiences into their lives. That is where these supplements come in because they assist us in revealing our inner truths to ourselves, and then acting in accordance with them.

Our DNA is permanently oscillating, winding and unwinding. Aulterra resonates with the DNA molecule and causes changes in its structure which creates constancy in the oscillation. This constancy causes a quantum shift in the DNA, which produces light energy in the cells.

Aulterra has been proven under scientific conditions to restore DNA and act in a similar way to hands-on healing in restoring the body's life force. It has been demonstrated to provide protection against electromagnetic pollution and is particularly beneficial to use when flying. It has also been demonstrated that Aulterra can improve the body's ability to utilise the nutrition within our foods. When many foods are lacking in the essential vitamins and minerals they once had, due to pollution and soil erosion, adding Aulterra to our foods can increase the amount of nutritional uptake we receive. As the recommended dose is only an eighth of a teaspoon, this is easily added to our foods. The Aulterra has to actually mix with the food to have the desired effect, it does not work if taken separately. Add Aulterra to each and every recipe in this book to really notice the power of Raw Magic!

Clearly, the monatomic trace elements are not a magical cure-all. It is not as easy as taking them and suddenly becoming realigned in body and mind, instantly transformed into a spiritually enlightened being. But they provide a doorway. At every moment in life we are making choices, consciously and very often unconsciously. We make decisions on what is possible and what is permissible based on past experience, and very often these foundations are fear, hurt, judgement and loss. Taking the Etheriums keeps the other doorway open too: the doorway of love, joy, freedom and infinite possibility. Sometimes we cannot even see that doorway; sometimes we can see it but it seems too far away to step through. But it is massively helpful just to keep it open for when you are ready. This is why some people can take Etheriums and not notice any difference at first; it can take months before deep set patterns are dissolved. When I first took Etherium gold it had no noticeable effect on me, and I didn't take it again for a couple of years. Now I notice it instantly because I am in the right place in my life to step through that doorway.

www.harmonicinnerprizes.com
www.subtleenergies.com/ormus

Hemp and flax

Hemp and flax are the superfats. They are the only two vegetable fats that contain all three of the omega oils, the Essential Fatty Acids.

EFAs are fats which the body cannot make but which are essential for good health. The two major EFAs are omega 3 (linoleic acid) and omega 6 (alpha-linolenic acid). You can also get EFAs from fish, but many people choose not to eat animals for ethical reasons, plus there are issues with the levels of toxicity in fish oils. EFAs work wonders for the brain, which is made of over 60 per cent fat, and are excellent for the skin, as they increase the fluidity of the cell membrane.

Studies have shown that taking EFAs on a daily basis improves brain function; for instance the Durham trial in 2002 demonstrated remarkable results for the 100 school children who were given a fish oil supplement daily for six months. There was a noticeable improvement in concentration, learning ability and behaviour from the children who had the fish oil in contrast to the children who had the placebo.

EFAs are also often used to treat skin problems like eczema and psoriasis, both as an external application in skin creams and oils, and when taken internally. They are a

fantastic source of antioxidants, an essential nutrient for oxygenating the blood and preventing free radical damage. Other benefits associated with increased intake of EFAs include: an improvement in stamina and energy levels; a lowering of the risk of cardiovascular disease; metabolism balance and weight management; and an improvement in gut function.

Healthy fats are essential

In the West over the past few decades a low-fat diet has been seen as a healthy diet. However, the tide of public opinion is beginning to turn and people are realising this is a misconception. The raw food diet is actually a relatively *high* fat diet. Fats are essential to the body to metabolise foods; if we are always starved of them the body is permanently on alert and stores fat deposits in the cells, making the weight harder to shift. A diet abundant in healthy fats, however, means the body always feels nourished and so does not need to hoard excess fat in the same way. Fat nourishes the cell membranes and makes us shiny; healthy fats make us glow with inner radiance. Healthy fats include olives, avocados, durian, nuts, and seeds (although nuts should be eaten in moderation because they are mucus-forming and acidic).

Hemp contains omega 3, 6, and 9 oils in the perfect ratio for humans. Flax, on the other hand, has a higher proportion of omega 3s which is the one that is harder to find in the diet, and the one most of us are lacking in. If you are new to these oils and are only going to take one, I would advise starting with flax to correct the balance in your body. But once you have upped your levels suitably you can switch between either. Flax has a rich buttery flavour and a beautiful golden colour; hemp is green and has a more distinctive nutty taste.

People often ask if you cannot just eat the seeds, which are much cheaper than the pressed oils. Your body will extract some fats from the whole seed, but for most of us our bodies are not working at their most efficient and will not be able to metabolise the seed effectively. EFAs are so important, and most of us are so depleted in them, I feel it is important to take the oil in its pure form and make sure the body is getting what it needs. But we also enjoy the whole seed for its nutritional content as well as taking the oil every day. Both hemp oil and flax oil are unstable, which means they don't like being exposed to heat and light and go rancid easily. Never cook with them! Buy only oils in dark glass jars and store them in the fridge.

Hemp

Hemp is definitely in my top five most amazing foods on the planet. For a start, it loves Mother Gaia! It grows easily almost anywhere and is so hardy it needs no pesticides and chemicals, unlike cotton. Its growth as a crop nourishes the soil rather than depleting it, and benefits the environment by pulling carbon out of the air, making it the ideal food for sustainable farming.

As well as being mega-nutritious it is a great textile, makes beautiful paper, and is one of the best things you can put on your skin. THC, the psychoactive constituent in marijuana, is negligible in hemp grown for commercial uses. Most hemp comes from China or Canada; the hemp that is grown in Canada has the highest GLA content – hemp is the only plant source of gamma-linoliec acid.

"Make the most you can of the Indian hemp seed, and sow it everywhere."
– George Washington
(who was a hemp farmer)

Hemp seed comes in three forms: whole, hulled and protein powder. The whole seeds are a lot more nutritious because they have been left intact. When ground up and eaten fresh they are wonderful because the shells crack and the amazing properties of the oil are delivered straight to you. However, many people find the grittiness of the shells unpalatable. I like to use them in recipes in small amounts to add flavour and texture, but not solely as they can be overpowering. The hulled seeds are the seeds with their shells removed and far more tasty and appealing, but will have lost some of their vitality and nutrients in the hulling process. They are small and white and soft, and much more popular, as they make wonderful smooth raw creams.

Hemp protein powder is the seed with the fat extracted. This makes it exceptionally high in protein (about 50 per cent). It has a deep earthy flavour, which goes equally well in sweet and savoury dishes. I often add it to sauces and dressings for extra bulk, and it's commonly used in smoothies. Hemp protein powder is favoured by athletes, and is also an excellent supplement for growing children. Hemp contains the full spectrum of amino acids, making it one of the few vegetable foods that is a complete protein, and furthermore the amino acids are in the perfect ratios for humans. It is also an excellent source of trace minerals, particularly magnesium. Add all this together and you have one of the most nutritional plants on the planet.

Flax

Flaxseeds or linseeds come from a herb which has also been popular historically as a fabric – this is where the name linen comes from. Flax oil is great used as a skin rub, to absorb the EFAs directly through the skin. I

"Wherever flaxseed becomes a regular food item among the people, there will be better health." – Mahatma Gandhi also always put flax or hemp oil into my enema water to get my EFAs direct through the colon wall. Flax oil has many health benefits: it has been shown to decrease blood pressure, has anti-inflammatory and anti-viral properties, and enhances the immune system. Flax is a very strange seed that acts unlike any others. It must be eaten either finely ground or soaked to receive the health benefits.

When it is milled it should be eaten fresh before the oils start to decay. In this form it acts as a thickening agent in recipes: one tablespoon of ground flaxseed mixed with three tablespoons of water is equivalent to one egg as a coagulator. It is often used in raw food cuisine as a binder for burgers and loaves. When soaked it forms a gloopy mass, a bit like frogspawn. It's not very palatable like this but extremely health-giving and a great digestive aid, acting as an intestinal broom and helping with IBS. One cup of flaxseeds soaked overnight will absorb 3-4 cups water.

www.durhamtrial.org
www.yaoh.co.uk
www.udoerasmus.com

Coconut

The coconut is actually a fruit, growing mainly in South East Asia. It is a great source of protein, fats, vitamins and minerals: particularly potassium, calcium, sodium and magnesium. It is a unique fat and especially valuable to vegans and raw fooders.

When we start to cut out the denser foods from our diets like wheat and dairy products, we still crave heavier things to keep us grounded. The tendency is to reach for nuts which are fibrous, and hard work for the digestion. Too many nuts are mucus-forming, acidic and put the body out of balance. Coconuts on the other hand put less strain on the liver and pancreas while still managing to get those denser fats into the diet.

Coconut is one of the few plant sources of saturated fats. Coconuts have had a bad press for a long time because it was assumed that all saturated fats were unhealthy, but the saturated fats in coconut do not raise cholesterol or contribute to heart disease.

The fats in coconut oil are medium chain fatty acids. Medium chain fatty acids are burned up quickly in the body, but long chain fatty acids get stored. Hence medium chain fatty acids are a better source of energy and help with weight loss. Lauric acid is an essential fatty acid which is gaining wide recognition as being as important in the diet as the omega oils. Coconut is the only plant source of lauric acid, which has anti-viral, anti-bacterial and anti-microbial properties. It can help the body deal with fungal infections, prevent viruses, and generally boost the immune system.

Breast milk is the only substance which has a greater concentration of lauric acid, which is why coconuts are a great thing to give to babies when you are weaning. When I drink coconut water, I imagine that's how breast milk must taste – sweet, nurturing, refreshing, energising, calming, balancing, all at once! Coconuts are similar in shape to a woman's breast, so I like to think of coconut water as Mother Earth's breast milk.

Coconut oil is also the only fat which is heat stable, so it is the best for cooking with. All other fats oxidise when heated and become toxic to the body. Coconut is a great food for balancing the metabolism. Like cacao it seems to regulate the body's natural appetite and assist the body in maintaining its ideal weight. It promotes healthy thyroid function and so can be very beneficial for people with both under-active and over-active thyroid conditions. There is evidence that it can help the body fight candida, IBS, Crohn's disease, diabetes, chronic fatigue, cancer, and HIV.

Like hemp and flax, the coconut plant has a multitude of uses. The matting from the outer skin is known as coir and is has a variety of uses such as ropes, mats and brushes. The shells are made into household tools, drums and buttons. Coconut oil is one of the best things you can put on the skin and is popular as a natural lubricant.

Consuming coconuts

There are many different ways to consume coconut. The best way is to travel to Asia and eat the fresh coconuts from the tree!

Young or jelly coconuts can often be found at festivals or Asian grocers, and are far superior to the brown ones in taste and nutrition. They are picked fresh off the coconut palm before they are fully ripe. To eat them, hack off the top with a machete or very sharp knife. Drink the water and scoop out the jelly-like flesh with a spoon, which is much thinner and softer than the brown nuts. A large nut should provide around one litre of water. You can blend the flesh and water up together to make amazing raw coconut milk.

Mature coconuts are the brown ones found at coconut shys or in supermarkets. They have ripened and fallen off the tree naturally. The flesh is much harder than that of young coconuts and they contain less liquid. To eat, make a hole in the eyes with a screwdriver, and pour out the liquid into a glass. Then smash the coconut open with a hammer, and prise out the flesh with a knife or screwdriver. Wear gloves to protect your hands! Store the pieces in the fridge and they'll keep for two or three days. We find they make a tasty and filling snack instead of biscuits or sweets.

The coconut oil/butter market exploded in the UK in 2005 as news of its weight-loss and health-giving properties reached the mainstream. Now there are many brands of good quality butter available. Look for ones which are virgin cold-pressed. Coconut butter and oil are the same thing; coconut melts at temperatures of 76 °F, so in cold weather it is solid, and in the summer it goes liquid. In the UK it is more often butter and in the US more commonly oil! This property makes it perfect for sweet and cake making, because when melted it blends easily into other ingredients and then can be hardened in the fridge to form solid sweets and cakes without cooking.

Coconut water is popular as a sports drink because it balances the electrolytes in the body. You can buy coconut water in cartons ready to drink. Look for the unpasteurised brands like Dr Martins. It is a brilliant source of minerals, vitamins and antioxidants. It is fantastic after exercise or cycling. It's also a wonderful first drink for babies to help wean them off the breast.

Coconut chips are generally heat-treated for a few minutes to preserve them, so they are not technically raw. We use them in trail mixes, or sometimes blend them up to make a cream.

Creamed coconut comes in blocks. It is the fat made from blending coconut water and flesh, and then heating it and allowing the fat to separate.

Coconut milk comes in tins and is made by blending the flesh and water and then pasteurising it to preserve it.

Desiccated coconut is traditionally the most well-known form of coconut in the UK, used as a cake and sweet decoration.

Coconuts are a part of my daily diet and I find them to be a great source of clean energy. They satiate me without leaving me feeling heavy or dull, and are one of my main calorific sources of fuel. They give me a sustained and calm boost, particularly when combined with maca. We use them mostly in sweet and cake making, but also in sauces and puddings to add creaminess and richness.

www.coconut-connections.com

I am so excited about superfoods in the kitchen. I am a fervent believer that super-foods are not just for smoothies. These are *foods* not supplements, and if you want to include them on a daily basis I believe it is wise to integrate them into your existing menus rather than try and add new things, which can cause confusion to your routine and overload your body.

A sustainable healthy diet is low in sugars, so I have invented tons of recipes to get your superfoods into your savoury dishes. There are enough recipes here that you could eat chocolate every day without having any sugars at all! On the other hand, I have also included an abundance of sweet treats too. There are cakes, sweets and puddings galore, many of which contain more nutrition than the average square meal.

This is not just healthy food, this is the best food ever!

This food is so good it is off the scale, in a class of its own. You can indulge yourself in the yummiest things you have ever eaten, you will not feel an ounce of suffering or denial, and you will have more energy and enthusiasm for life than you have ever had! Grand claims? Try it for yourself, what have you got to lose? A few pounds, an annoying partner, a job you don't like? This is the food of the revolution, food that will change your life, to give you the joy and vitality to make all your dreams come true. You might be saying, "Oh, I like my life, I am happy the way I am." Well, that's even more exciting. I liked my life before I started eating superfoods, I was really happy the way I was, I liked myself, my family, my friends, my work. But you know what? Since I started eating these foods daily, my world has shifted into a whole new orbit. Everything is possible because I am the creator of my own reality, and the reality I am creating is so good.

Eating superfoods helps us be the very best we can be, and every day just gets better. Life is an infinite and abundant path of reflection, inspiration, motivation, positive action, and integration.

Ecstatic bliss becomes the norm

Shall I repeat that? Existence is ecstasy. Our natural state of being is to be as free as the birds, as wise as the horses, as rooted as the trees, as expansive as the mountains, and when we clear our lives of the clutter and debris which cloud our bodies and minds, we tune into the majesty and beauty of the earth and reclaim the magic which is our birthright.

Every recipe in this book has been invented and tested and retested at least three times. So they definitely work!

We have made measuring as simple as we can. You can either use cups, or grams and litres. A lot of the recipes call for tablespoons – an English tablespoon is not the same as an American tablespoon. So if you are working according to American measurements, remember where I say one tablespoon that's the equivalent of three teaspoons.

Chef's notes

Buckwheaties

We use buckwheat a lot – in cereal, mixed into chocolate, and ground into flour for crusts and cakes. 300g (2 cups buckwheat) makes 450g (3 cups) buckwheaties. Put your buckwheat in a large bowl, cover it with water, and give it a good swish around. Drain it, then cover it in water again and leave it soaking for five hours – no more than eight hours max. Drain, and rinse once more. Leave it in the bowl to sprout for two or three days, giving it a rinse and a swish once a day. Once it's sprouted – with tails about the same size as the seed and no longer – spread it over drying trays and put it in the dehydrator for twelve hours. Stored in an airtight container it will keep for a couple of months. Raw Living sells ready-made Buckwheaties.

Melting butters

A lot of the recipes call for melted cacao butter and/or coconut butter. We've found the easiest way to do it is with a porringer: a double saucepan that you can buy through our website. If you don't have a double saucepan, boil some water in a kettle or a pan. Then stand the butter in its jar in the pan, or transfer just what you need to a bowl, and stand that in the pan. In warmer weather you don't need to melt the coconut butter, it will be runny enough to use straight from the cupboard. If it's really hot you don't need to melt the cacao butter either.

Salt

Some of the recipes include tamari or miso as salt substitutes. I generally put a pinch of Himalayan crystal salt in everything I make, sweet or savoury – it brings out the flavours and aids absorption of the minerals. Celtic sea salt is good too. I haven't put it in the recipes but keep some to hand, because life is always best when taken with a pinch of salt.

Adding water gradually

When blending, it's vital to add the water gradually. If you pour it all in at the beginning of the recipe with all the other ingredients, it will not get amalgamated properly and the end result will be runny. Add the water slowly, little by little: if you're using a cup of water (250ml), add it a quarter of a cup at a time, blending as you go, and then your finished recipe will be the right thickness.

Weighing avocados

Weights given are for whole avocados, including the skin and stones, not just the flesh. I've done this because avocados vary so much in size, when you're using more than one or two it's usually safer going by weight than by counting avocados.

Etheriums

Where a recipe calls for one of the monatomic trace elements, this is for its energetic properties only and does not affect the taste. If you want to leave them out or substitute one for another it's not going to affect the recipe working in the slightest, only the alchemical effects. The same goes for suma.

Sweeteners

My preferred sweeteners, which I have used mostly in the book, are lucuma, mesquite, agave nectar, and xylitol. Lucuma is a powder made from a Peruvian fruit similar to a mango. It has a beautiful biscuitty flavour. Mesquite is another powder, made from a pod similar to carob. It has a sweeter, more caramelly flavour than carob. You can buy them from Detox Your World or Raw Living, or use carob powder as a substitute. Agave nectar is a syrup made from the same cactus plant that tequila is extracted from. It's the best quality raw syrup around, but if you can't get it you can substitute your preferred sweetener like maple or rice syrup, or raw honey. Xylitol is made from fermented birch bark, and it's a low glycaemic, healthy alternative to sugar. Some people are suspicious of it because it looks quite processed, but I have found a few spoonfuls in recipes is a great way to increase the sweetness without adding too much bulk. There are a few makes on the market, but we generally use Higher Nature's Xylitol.

Vegans

Strict vegans avoid the use of bee products. All the recipes in this book are vegan apart from those that include honey or bee pollen. Where honey is used, vegans can always substitute agave nectar. Bee pollen can be substituted with hulled hemp seeds.

Equipment

There are a few basic pieces of equipment that I use time and time again for my recipes. If you have all these in your kitchen you'll be able to recreate everything in this book.

Blender

A really good blender makes all the difference to your ability to turn out fine raw cuisine. The VitaMix is the raw connoisseur's blender of choice but unfortunately it's a little over-priced at £400 odd. It does do everything though – blend to within an inch of your life, and grind nuts and seeds to fine powders. If you haven't got a high-power blender you need to be a bit inventive with a combination of a hand-held blender, a coffee grinder or spice mill attachment which comes with most blenders, and a food processor. And you still need a blender.

Dehydrator

If you're a raw fooder it's pretty likely that you'll have one of these already. They make raw crackers, biscuits, cookies and breads so good you'll never miss the cooked versions. If you don't have one you can try using your oven on the lowest possible setting – the results aren't quite the same, but they're passable.

Porringer

We use this for melting coconut and cacao butter – it's a double saucepan. If you don't have one you need a saucepan and a Pyrex bowl that fits neatly inside it.

Cake tins

There are two types of cake in this book: one calls for a flan tin, 9.5 in/24 cm in diameter. The other needs a springform cake tin, 7.5 in/20 cm in diameter. They're both easy to find in cook shops.

Trays

You need a selection of trays for making chocolate and fudge, in two basic sizes. You can use Tupperware, baking trays or ceramic trays. Where I state "medium-sized", the optimum is about 15 cm (6 in) square, and a large tray needs to be about half as big again (about 15 cm x 23 cm or 6 in x 9 in).

Cutlery

You need a couple of good tablespoons that you can always find when you need them, a heap of teaspoons, and a good chopping knife. Forks come in handy for digging coconut butter out of the jars and ground cacao nibs out of the bottom of the blender.

Big fridge

Hell yeah. Preferably pink. Or silver. If it's white you need to cover it in stickers, magnets, and postcards.

Note to American readers

The UK and USA definitions of a tablespoon are different. In this book:

One tablespoon = 3 teaspoons

Dips and dressings are central to raw food cuisine. Having a selection of favourites in the fridge makes meal times easy and fast.

- Serve a dollop with crudités – don't just stick to carrots and celery, try red pepper, broccoli florets, cauliflower florets, fennel strips, courgette sticks, chicory leaves, turnip slices, mooli sticks, apple; be adventurous with your combinations and surprise your taste buds.
- Use in a wrap – nori sheets, cabbage leaves or romaine lettuce leaves make the best outer layers. If you're enthusiastic and you have a dehydrator, you can make lovely raw wraps with sprouted buckwheat or flaxseed. Stuff your wrap with pate and sprouts, and munch away to your heart's content.
- Spread them on bread and crackers, raw or otherwise.
- Dips and pates can be thinned out to make salad dressings. Add a little water or extra oil, get some good quality green leaves, preferably organic, local and seasonally grown, and voila. A plate of rocket, half an avocado, a handful of sprouts, a sprinkle of cacao nibs, and a tasty dressing and you have a meal fit for royalty in less than minutes.

Most recipes given make enough for four to six servings, so you can make a batch, keep it in the fridge, and it should last you half a week.

You need a good blender to make most of these dishes. A normal high street blender will do the job, but for really professional results a high-speed blender is a fantastic investment. You can make do fine without one, but if you get one, you'll be really glad of it, it makes everything quicker, easier and tastier.

Cacaomole

Serves 2
10 mins
Blender

This is one of my favourite lunches. Spread on a nori sheet and rammed with alfalfa sprouts, you couldn't fit any more nutrition in each bite. If you don't have a blender, you can still make this, just crush the garlic by hand, and mash everything up with a fork.

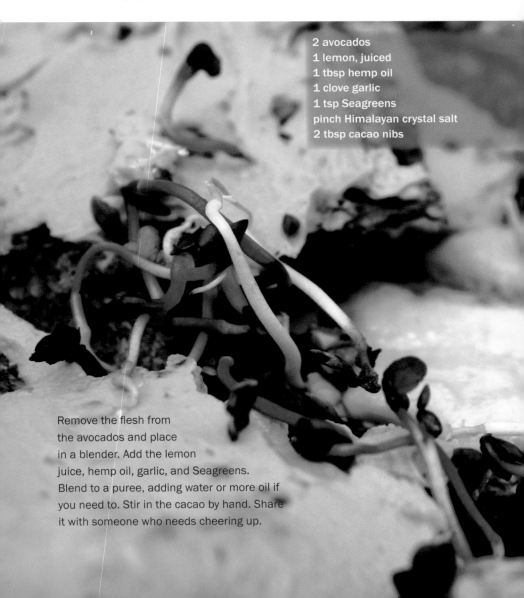

2 avocados
1 lemon, juiced
1 tbsp hemp oil
1 clove garlic
1 tsp Seagreens
pinch Himalayan crystal salt
2 tbsp cacao nibs

Remove the flesh from the avocados and place in a blender. Add the lemon juice, hemp oil, garlic, and Seagreens. Blend to a puree, adding water or more oil if you need to. Stir in the cacao by hand. Share it with someone who needs cheering up.

Hempamole

Serves four
10 mins
Blender

Having one of those days? Hempamole on *Fire wizard crackers* (p158) topped with alfalfa sprouts and a pinch of crystal manna will help you over any hump.

2 avocados
2 tomatoes
1 red chilli
2 lemons, juiced
4 tbsp hemp protein powder
1 clove garlic
1 tsp miso
2 tbsp hemp oil
2 tbsp dehulled hemp seeds
1 tbsp Seagreens

Remove the flesh from the avocados and put it in the blender. Remove the stalks from the tomatoes, quarter them, and put them in the blender too. Remove the stalks and seeds from the chilli and add that to the blender. Next add the lemon juice, hemp protein, garlic, miso and hemp oil and blend it all together to a thick cream. Stir in the hemp seeds and Seagreens by hand.

Bee's knees guacamole

Serves four
10 mins
Blender

Pollen and spices complement each other really well – this is guacamole with a sting. We buy organic curry paste, but you can use whatever you have in the cupboard.

2 avocados
2 tomatoes
2 tbsp apple cider vinegar
1 clove garlic
2 tsp curry paste
100 g or 1 cup bee pollen
4 tbsp dulse flakes

Remove the flesh from the avocados and put it in the blender. Quarter the tomatoes and add those in with the vinegar, garlic clove and curry paste. Blend to a thick cream. By hand, stir in the bee pollen and dulse flakes. Keeps in the fridge for up to a week, and actually improves after a day or two as the pollen starts to dissolve into the guacamole.

Hempiness hummusness

Serves six
10 mins, 8-12 hrs pre-soaking
Blender

The combination of whole and hulled hemp seeds ensures you get a good dose of those essential fatty acids. The action of the blender cracks open the seeds and means you get the full effect of those wonderful oils.

Pre-soak the sesame seeds and hemp seeds together in a bowl, preferably overnight. When you're ready to use them, drain them and rinse them. Chuck everything in the blender along with a half cup of the water. Turn the blender on and add the remaining half a cup of water a little at a time, until you have the desired consistency — a creamy, hummus-like paste. Can be served immediately or stored in a jar in the fridge for up to a week.

150 g or 1 ½ cups hulled sesame seeds, soaked 8-12 hrs
50 g or ½ cup hulled hemp seeds, soaked 8-12 hrs
60 g or ½ cup whole hemp seeds, soaked 8-12 hrs
1 lemon, juiced
2 tbsp hemp oil
1 clove garlic
1 tsp tamari
250 ml or 1 cup pure water

Crazy carrot relish

This is ridiculously good as an accompaniment to a salad or piled on top of crackers.

Serves four
10 mins
Grater

Grate the carrot and transfer to a mixing bowl. Finely dice the onion and put that in the bowl too. Add the pollen, flax oil and curry paste and give it all a good stir together.

100 g or 2 large carrots, grated
¼ red onion
50 g or ½ cup pollen
1 tbsp flax oil
1 tsp curry paste

Greenvy

Serves four
10 mins
Blender

Like gravy but green, I love this dip for its appley shade and delicate flavour. Hulled sesame is not so nutritious as the whole seed, but it makes a much tastier cream. Use as a dip for crudités, or add a little water to thin and use as an alkalising dressing for green salad leaves.

125 g or 1 cup hulled sesame seeds
1 tbsp olive oil
1 tbsp apple cider vinegar
2 tbsp barleygrass
½ tsp crystal salt
250 ml or 1 cup water

Put all the ingredients together in the blender with half the water. Add the rest of the water gradually while the blender is running, and blend for a few minutes until it makes a thick cream. Will keep in the fridge for up to a week.

Greyvy

Like greenvy, but grey. We use this as a gravy for green vegetables like broccoli, peas, and sauerkraut. It's so tasty you can pour it liberally over your veg for a satisfying quick tea.

Put all the ingredients in the blender, with half the water. Blend to a cream so that the hemp seeds are completely amalgamated. Add the rest of the water gradually, with the blender running until it reaches the desired consistency. Will thicken a little if left in the fridge.

125 g or 1 cup hemp seeds hulled
2 tbsp tahini
4 tbsp hemp protein
1 tbsp hemp sauce
1 tbsp kelp
4 tbsp hemp oil
250 ml or 1 cup water

Chocolate mayonnaise

Wow! I don't know what else to say. Just, wow. Use as a dip, or thin for a dressing. Goes great on seaweeds.

Serves four

10 mins

Blender

Put all the ingredients in the blender with half the water. Blend to a thick cream, then add the rest of the water gradually with the blender running until you have a thick dollopy consistency.

250 g or 2 cups hulled hemp seeds
50 g or ½ cup cacao nibs
1 tbsp tamari
1 t bsp olive oil
1 lemon, juiced
1 clove garlic
250 ml or 1 cup water

Cranberry and goji relish

Serves four
10 mins
Blender

Perfect at Christmas with your *Omega love loaf* (p161) and Brussel sprout *Cacaoslaw* (p123).

3 tomatoes
100 g or 1 cup fresh cranberries
50 g or ½ cup goji berries
50 g or ½ cup dried cranberries
¼ onion
½ chilli
1 tsp apple cider vinegar

Put everything in the blender and blend for a few minutes. Will thicken when left in the fridge.

Goji ketchup

Serves eight
10 mins, pre-soaking 30 mins
Blender

This is so popular, a sweet tangy relish that is perfect for children. Usually we just eat it as it is, with some green crudités like broccoli, cucumber and celery.

3 large tomatoes
100 g or 1 cup gojis
50 g or ½ cup sun-dried tomatoes, pre-soaked 30 mins
¼ red onion
1 tbsp olive oil
1 tbsp apple cider vinegar
1 tsp tamari

Soak the tomatoes for 30 minutes in the purest water available. When they're ready, drain them and put everything in the blender together. Blend for a couple of minutes until you have a smooth puree. Keeps well for up to a week in the fridge.

Greatest garlic goji relish

Serves eight
10 mins
Blender

Everyone adores this, especially children. It's one of my most popular dips, with an amazing fruity flavour you know is filling your cells with fun.

Chop the red pepper into pieces big enough for your blender, carefully removing all the seeds. Put everything in the blender together and blend til the gojis are mashed and there's no bits left. Keeps in the fridge for up to a week.

200 g or 1 red pepper
100 g or 1 cup gojis
2 tbsp apple cider vinegar
2 cloves garlic
½ tsp salt

Broccoli bonkers

Serves four
10 mins
Blender

This is a greener than green dip for when life gets a bit too bonkers and you need reassuring that at least your dinner makes sense, if nothing else.

250 g or 1 small head broccoli
¼ red onion
2 tbsp spirulina
2 tbsp olive oil
2 lemons, juiced
1 tbsp nutritional yeast flakes
1 tbsp tahini
1 tbsp Seagreens

Chop the broccoli into small pieces to fit into your blender. Put all the ingredients apart from the Seagreens into the blender together, and give it a good going until it's creamy. If it's too much like hard work for your blender, you can add a little water or some extra oil. Once it's turning over and there are no lumps of broccoli left, stir in the Seagreens by hand. Keeps for a few days, or you can dehydrate leftovers and crumble them into croutons for salad.

Spread it on your bread

Serves four
5 mins
No equipment needed

We love tahini on our bread, but too much of it is heavy on the liver and mucus-forming. So we add lemon juice to create more of a balance. When you mix lemon juice into tahini it has a thickening effect, so you also need to add a lot of water. This way, you're making your tahini go twice as far! Aulterra increases the absorption of nutrients in the food; we often add it to salads and dips.

Put everything but the water in a small bowl and mix together with a teaspoon. When you have a thick paste add the water, a spoon at a time, until you reach the desired consistency.

2 tbsp tahini
1 lemon, juiced
2 tsp miso
1 tbsp flax oil
½ tsp Aulterra
4 tbsp water

Purple pesto

8 servings
10 mins
Blender

This pesto is such a beautiful colour. It's gorgeous spread thinly on crackers or used as salad dressing for some purple leaves like oakleaf or radicchio.

1 large bunch basil
100 g or ¾ cup hulled hemp seeds
1 clove garlic
2 tbsp olive oil
2 tbsp apple cider vinegar
1 tbsp agave nectar
1 tsp purple corn extract
1 tsp white miso

Prepare the basil for the blender. You can use most of it, though you may want to discard some of the ends if they are very thick and woody. Put everything in the blender together, and blend until you have a gorgeous thick paste.

Magic maca pesto

Serves four
5 mins
Blender

Maca works equally well in savoury and sweet dishes, adding an interesting flavour and energising your food. This works as a dip or a dressing.

1 large bunch basil
100 g or 1 cup sesame seeds
50 g or ½ cup maca
4 tbsp hemp oil
1 tbsp agave nectar
1 tbsp apple cider vinegar
1 tbsp tamari
1 clove garlic

Prepare the basil for the blender, removing any exceptionally thick stems. Put everything in the blender together with half the water and blend to a paste. Add the rest of the water gradually while the blender turns, until you have a thick cream.

Magic maca pesto

Many ways mayonnaise

Serves eight
10 mins
Blender

This is a perfect staple to keep in the fridge for dipping, dressing, spreading, dehydrating, spooning, licking, sucking... now I'm just getting carried away.

200 g or 1¾ cups hulled hemp seeds
50 g or ½ cup maca
1 tsp Aulterra
¼ tsp crystal salt
2 tbsp olive oil
2 lemons, juiced
1 clove garlic
250 ml or 1 cup water

Put everything except the water in the blender. Blend together for a minute, then add the water gradually while the blender is turning. Keep in the fridge – it doesn't keep well, eat within a few days.

Mayo maynot

Serves four
10 mins, 3 hrs setting
Blender

This has all the over-richness of traditional mayonnaise
that makes you want to dip it in chips and forget about
your thighs in a few moments of unmeasured ecstasy. But because, as we all know
by now, coconut butter balances your metabolism and so doesn't make you put on
weight, you can eat this safe in the knowledge that you can have both unmeasured
ecstasy and divine thighs.

100 g or 1 cup coconut butter
2 tbsp miso
3 lemon, juiced
100 g or ½ cup tahini
125 ml or ½ cup water

Melt the coconut butter in a bowl over a pan of boiled
water. Blend everything together. Leave in the fridge to
set, although you can eat it as it is, warm and dribbly.

Gardner Street dressing

Serves four

10 mins

No equipment needed

When we had the Raw Magic shop, Alxxx used to go to Infinity wholefoods and buy greens and avocado. Then we'd hide behind the counter and make this in paper water cups with plastic spoons, mix it all up in a big bowl with some Sunseeds and cacao nibs out of the pick-and-mix, and feed each other. A customer would come in and we'd sit there with purple and green mouths, trying to look all innocent. Which we're both quite good at.

Put everything in a bowl (or a paper cup) apart from the water. Stir it with a spoon until it's evenly mixed. It looks a bit of a boring brown colour but taste it and you'll be amazed at how lively it is. Add the water gradually until you reach the desired consistency for your dressing.

2 tbsp barleygrass
1 tbsp tahini
1 tbsp flax oil
1 lemon, juiced
½ tsp crystal salt
½ tsp purple corn extract
4 tbsp water

Macand of dressing

Serves four
5 mins
No equipment needed

This is my kind of dressing: simple but decadent. It makes a beautifully easy dinner poured over a pile of green leaves like rocket, baby leaf spinach and corn salad.

1 tbsp tahini
2 tbsp hemp oil
1 tbsp maca powder
1 tsp white miso
½ lemon, juiced
60 ml or ¼ cup water

Put all the ingredients except the water into a small bowl. Gradually pour in the water, stirring as you add it. Once you have a creamy thin sauce, it is ready. You can store leftovers in the fridge, but maca doesn't keep well once mixed with water; eat within a few days.

Finest flax

Serves six
10 mins
Blender

You're best off using this dressing straight away – if it sits in the fridge, the flax seeds will swell and absorb the oil so it's more gloopy. If that happens just give it a good stir and maybe blend in some extra lemon juice and water if you want it runnier, although I like it the way it is – it coats the salad in a kind of clumpy fashion…

Grind the flax in a coffee mill or high power blender. Put everything together in the blender and blend until you've got a gloop.

75 g or ½ cup flax seeds, ground
125 ml or ½ cup flax oil
½ tsp crystal salt
2 lemons, juiced

Tim's dressing

Serves four
10 mins
Blender

This is another one of those super ideas to have hiding in the fridge, ready to do exciting things with when you get in at 7pm and haven't got many brain cells left. Pour it over leaves, grated carrot, finely chopped broccoli, anything and everything that's loitering in your fridge drawers and hey presto, instant dinner manifestation. It's named after Tim of Yaoh, the UK's leading hemp hero.

125 g or 1 cup hulled hemp seeds
125 ml or ½ cup olive oil
2 tbsp brown rice vinegar
2 tbsp hemp sauce

Put everything in the blender and keep going for a minute or so until it's creamy. If you can't be bothered to blend the sauce, you can omit the hulled hemp seeds and just make a vinaigrette.

5
Salads and
Savouries

In case you hadn't got the message by now, I am truly passionate about getting you to put superfoods in your dinner.

I think it's important that we use them as any other kitchen ingredient, like vegetables and herbs, rather than reserving them for special occasions or only putting them into sweets and smoothies. They shouldn't be considered as supplements, they are foods, and if we want to really experience the benefits we need to integrate them into our existing menus and make sure we get plenty every day, at every meal. This is a whole new way of eating, that will bring a whole new dimension of pleasure to your mealtimes.

Start eating the Raw Magic way and life will never be the same again.

Cauliflower cream

Soothing and nurturing, kind of like mashed potato.
If you try it and you don't like it, or you've got some
leftovers, you can spread it onto dehydrator trays to make good crackers.

Pre-soak the flaxseeds in the water for at
least three hours. They will absorb all or
most of the water – don't throw any away.
Put the cauliflower, tahini, lemon juice, miso,
garlic and kelp in the blender with the flaxseeds and blend to a smooth cream. After
a minute or two, once there are no lumps
of cauliflower left, stir in the Seagreens by
hand: then it's ready. Eat the same day.

75 g or ½ cup flaxseeds, pre-soaked
200 ml or ¾ cup water
200 g or ½ cauliflower
2 tbsp tahini
2 lemons, juiced
2 tsp miso
1 clove garlic
1 tsp kelp

Naughty noodles

Serves four

20 mins

Spiralizer or grater

A spiralizer is the raw fooder's favourite gadget for making raw noodles and pasta. They're inexpensive, easy to use, and fun to play with. If you haven't got one you can grate the squash instead; it's not the same effect but it still works.

Cut your squash into eight pieces: in half across the middle and the two halves into quarters lengthways. Scoop the seeds out of the bottom half. Place each piece in the spiralizer with the noodle setting on, or grate using a food processor. Transfer your noodles to a large mixing bowl. In a smaller bowl, use a spoon to blend the cacao powder, tahini, hemp oil, chilli powder, lemon juice, tamari and water. You should have quite a runny dressing. Pour this over the noodles with the nibs, hemp seeds, and dulse flakes. Give it all a good mix together so the dressing is evenly covering the noodles and there are no clumps left. Serve with a green salad and *Macand of dressing* (p112) or *Supersexy curry* (p122).

1 medium sized Butternut squash
4 tbsp cacao powder
2 tbsp tahini
2 tbsp hemp oil
1 tsp chilli powder
1 lemon, juiced
1 tbsp tamari
60 ml or ¼ cup water
2 tbsp cacao nibs
2 tbsp hulled hemp seeds
4 tbsp dulse flakes

Jonny's luminous soup

Serves two

Blender

10 mins

I read a lovely quote saying, "We have the ability to develop the luminous energy fields of angels within this lifetime." It became a running joke with Jonny and I – "I can't come to the phone, I'm just developing my luminous energy field," "I've forgotten what I was saying, I got distracted by developing my luminous energy field," that kind of thing. So this is *Jonny's luminous soup*, specially designed to help you develop your very own luminous energy field.

Prepare the celery, cucumber, spinach and avocado for your blender by removing unwanted stems etc, and chopping them small enough that they won't cause trouble for your machine. Put them all in, along with the hemp oil and lemon juice. Blend to a liquid. Then add the broccoli, garlic, hemp seeds and barleygrass powder and blend again until you have a cream. Serve by warming gently, and garnish each bowl of soup with ¼ teaspoon crystal manna flakes.

2 sticks celery
1 cucumber
50 g or 1 cup spinach
250 g or 1 avocado
2 tbsp hemp oil
1 lemon, juiced
200 g or 2 cups broccoli florets
1 clove garlic
2 tbsp hulled hemp seeds
2 tbsp barleygrass powder
½ teaspoon crystal manna flakes

The Doxtor's ultimalkaliser soup

Serves two
Blender
10 mins

A cucumber a day keeps the Doxtor happy. This soup contains everything you need to alkalise and energise – all that cucumber, a generous serving of barleygrass and a sprinkling of nori flakes.

Chop the cucumbers into pieces which will go into your blender happily. Put them in with the hemp seeds, vinegar and salt, and give it a good blend until you have a liquid with no chunks of cucumber or bits of hemp seed left. Add the barleygrass and maca and give it another quick whiz. Warm gently if you like, and serve sprinkled with nori flakes.

1½ cucumbers
100 g or ¾ cup hulled hemp seeds
1 tbsp apple cider vinegar
½ tsp crystal salt
1 tbsp barleygrass
1 tbsp maca
1 tbsp nori flakes

Supersexy curry

Charged with superfoods, this dinner is perfect for feeding to your very own god or goddess.

1 large avocado
3 small tomatoes
2 sticks celery
¼ red onion
1 lemon, juiced
2 tbsp hulled hemp seeds
2 tsp curry powder
1 tbsp maca powder
¼ tsp suma powder
100 g or 1 cup cauliflower
½ red pepper
50 g or 1 cup spinach
1 tbsp goji berries

Peel and pit the avocado, and put the flesh into the blender. Halve the tomatoes and chop the celery sticks into eighths, and put them in the blender too. Add the onion, lemon juice, hemp seeds and curry powder and blend to a thick puree. Add in the maca and suma and blend briefly (if you blend maca for too long it goes bitter). Remove the sauce from the blender and put in a bowl. Chop your cauliflower into small bite-sized pieces, and dice your pepper into pieces the same size. Stir the cauliflower, pepper, spinach and gojis into the sauce. Eat straight away.

Cacaoslaw

Serves four

15 mins

Food processor, blender

Adding a sprinkle of cacao nibs to any salad lifts it to a whole new level. Coleslaw is such a basic it can become boring, but as you may have noticed by now, eat enough superfoods and the word "boring" starts to disappear from your vocabulary.

Top and tail the carrots. Quarter the apples and remove the core. Finely grate the carrots, apple, onion and cabbage. To make the mayonnaise, blend the avos, vinegar, salt, garlic, purple corn extract and water. Toss the vegetables in the mayonnaise, along with the nibs. This salad will keep for a day or two, and the vegetables will soften and the flavours improve.

2 carrots
1 apple
½ onion
200 g or 2 cups white cabbage
2 avocados
1 tbsp apple cider vinegar
pinch salt
1 clove garlic
1 tsp purple corn extract
125 ml or ½ cup water
75 g or ½ cup cacao nibs

Macauliflower cheese

This is a beautiful rich cheesy cream which is so good it might not actually make it onto the cauliflower. Don't worry if it doesn't, make some *Many ways mayonnaise* (p108) as well and use that instead.

125 g or 1 cup cashews, soaked 8-12 hrs
500 g or 1 cauliflower,
 divided into bite-sized florets
1 lemon, juiced
1 tsp white miso
2 tbsp nutritional yeast flakes
2 tbsp maca
250 ml or 1 cup water

Pre-soak the cashews overnight. Put the cashews, lemon juice, miso, nutritional yeast flakes and half the water in the blender and blend for a minute until there are no lumps of cashew left. Add in the maca, and as the blender turns add the rest of the water gradually. Chop the cauliflower into large bite-sized pieces, trying to preserve the florets as much as possible. Pour the sauce over the cauliflower, toss and serve. Eat within a day or two.

Cheeky chilli

I first made this on Christmas Day 2006. It's bright red because of the beetroot, and I served it with *Macauli-flower cheese* (p124) and *Christal kale* (p128), so the plates were a beautiful Christmassy red, white and green.

5 tomatoes
2 red chilli peppers
1 small bunch coriander
100 g or 1 cup goji berries
2 tbsp tamari
2 tbsp apple cider vinegar
4 tbsp olive oil
250 g or 4 small beetroot
2 carrots
100 g or 1 cup mixed beansprouts
100 g or ¾ cup cacao nibs

Chop the tomatoes into pieces small enough for your blender. Deseed the chilli. Loosely chop the coriander. Put the tomatoes, chilli and coriander in the blender with the gojis, tamari, vinegar, olive oil, and blend. Peel the beetroot, chop it into quarters, and use the S-blade on your food processor to process it into small pieces about the size of rice granules. Transfer the beetroot to a large mixing bowl. Top and tail the carrots, quarter them, and process in the same way. Transfer to the bowl with the beansprouts and cacao nibs and give it all a good stir together with a large spoon. Pour over the goji sauce and stir again so it is evenly mixed.

The orange orgasm

Serves four
15 mins
Blender

If you make this for a potential lover and he doesn't hoist you over his arm in a fireman's lift and carry you straight to the bedroom, then it's definitely time to give up, girls, and start looking around at some of the other fish in the sea.

100 g or ¾ cup cacao nibs
100 g or ¾ cup hulled hemp seeds
100 g or ¾ cup coconut butter
3 tomatoes
2 red peppers
½ red onion
1 red chilli pepper
50 g or ½ cup goji berries
2 tbsp dulse or dulse flakes
2 tsp tamari
1 tsp suma

Grind the nibs, hemp seeds and coconut butter together in the blender until you have a thick granular cream. Prepare the tomatoes, pepper, onion and chilli pepper for the blender. Make sure you remove all the seeds from the chilli pepper. Pop them in the blender with the goji berries, dulse, tamari and suma and blend again. Keep blending for a couple of minutes until you have a smooth orange cream. Serve accompanied by a green salad.

Crystal cumber number

Ooh baby, I've got your number. This dish is the epitome of what I am trying to convey with these dinners: so quick, so easy, inexpensive, and so nutritious you could live on it.

Serves two
10 mins
No equipment needed

Grind your flaxseeds if you haven't done so already. Cube the avocados into bite-sized pieces and spoon out the flesh into a mixing bowl. Cube the cucumber into pieces the same size and add them to the bowl. Stir in the Seagreens, crystal manna, flaxseed, flax oil and crystal salt. Make sure it's evenly mixed, and serve as a light lunch or tea.

3 tbsp flaxseed, ground
2 avocados
1 cucumber
1 tsp Seagreens
1 tsp crystal manna
1 tbsp flax oil
pinch crystal salt

127

Christal kale

Serves four
5 mins, 2 hrs marinating
No equipment needed

Dark, leafy green vegetables like kale and cavalo nero are about the best vegetables you can eat, especially when they're in season and locally grown. What the UK lacks in exotic fruits we more than make up for with the quality and variety of our greens. They're quite fibrous and chewy to eat just as they are raw, so rawfooders often use a technique called wilting, as described here. The presence of the oil also helps with the digestion of the kale. This is Chris's favourite, so I named it after him.

400 g or 8 cups or cavalo nero
3 tbsp olive oil
½ tsp crystal salt
2 avocados
4 tbsp dulse flakes
2 tbsp hulled hemp seeds
100 g or 1 cup Raw Living Sunseeds
2 tsp crystal manna

Chop the kale into small bite-sized pieces and transfer to a mixing bowl. Pour the olive oil over and sprinkle in the salt. With your hands, give the kale a good massage: rub the oil and salt right into the leaves. This softens and tenderizes them to make them more palatable. Massage the kale for a couple of minutes, then cube the avocado and add that into the mix with the dulse flakes, hemp seeds, Sunseeds (or alternatively a mixture of pumpkin and sunflower seeds), and one teaspoon crystal manna. Give it all a good mix and transfer to a large serving dish. Sprinkle the second teaspoon of crystal manna over the top evenly, then leave in the fridge for at least two hours to marinate. This dish keeps well for a couple of days.

Spaghetti gojous

Serves four
5 mins, 30 mins or more pre-soaking
No equipment needed

The fruitiness of the gojis complements the saltiness of the spaghetti really well in this dish. In Chinese cuisine, gojis are often used in chicken or duck dishes, and it is easy to see why once you start adding them into your dinners.

140 g (or 25 cm x 25 cm sheet) sea spaghetti
4 tbsp goji berries
4 tbsp hulled sesame seeds
1 tsp kelp
1 tbsp apple cider vinegar
4 tbsp olive oil
½ tsp crystal salt

Pre-soak the sea spaghetti for at least 30 mins, but preferably overnight. When it's ready, drain, and stir in all the other ingredients: then it's ready to serve. Will keep in the fridge for up to a week.

Balance your hempispheres salad

Serves two
10 mins
No equipment needed

If you can't get enough of hemp, this is the salad for you. Hemp comes to us in many forms, and this salad contains just about all of them. Serve with *Burger me* (p164) and *Hempilicious ice cream* (p186) for pudding and you'll be transported to hempiven.

50 g or 1 cup rocket
50 g or 1 cup baby leaf spinach
50 g or 1 cup corn salad
50 g or 1 cup alfalfa sprouts
100 g or 1 cup sauerkraut
2 tbsp cacao nibs
4 tbsp hulled hemp seeds
4 tbsp whole hemp seeds
2 tbsp hemp protein
1 avocado
2 tbsp hemp butter or omega butter
1 tbsp hemp oil
2 tsp hemp sauce
1 lemon, juiced

Put the rocket, spinach, corn salad, alfalfa, sauerkraut, cacao, hemp seeds (both types), and hemp protein in a salad bowl together. Cube the avocado flesh and add it to the salad. Give it all a good mix, so the sauerkraut and alfalfa are evenly threaded, not in clumps. In a separate small bowl, mix the hemp butter, hemp oil, hemp sauce and lemon juice with a spoon. You should have a runny paste to pour over your salad. As you toss the dressing in the salad, it will clump together into a dense mix. Serve immediately.

Sky high spaghetti

Serves four
5 mins, 30 mins or more pre-soaking
No equipment needed

My amazing friend Sky loves seaweed and he loves hemp, so this recipe is named after him. Hemp and seaweed are one of my favourite combinations: really earthing, calming and rebalancing.

Pre-soak the sea spaghetti for at least 30 mins, but the longer the better as far as this seaweed is concerned. When it's ready, drain and add all the other ingredients to the bowl. Give it a good stir and it's ready to serve. Will keep in the fridge for up to a week.

140 g (or 25 cm x 25 cm sheet) sea spaghetti
2 tbsp hulled hemp seeds
2 tbsp hemp protein powder
2 tbsp hemp oil
1 tbsp Seagreens
2 tsp hemp sauce

Multi-dimensional
sea vegetable salad

Serves four
5 mins, 20 mins or more pre-soaking
No equipment needed

We love Clearspring's Japanese sea salad.
It's a beautiful mix of green wakame, white agar, and a red seaweed called aka tsuno-
mata, so Ethan named it "Multi-coloured Sea Salad". We usually just add a simple
dressing to it, and eat it as it is.

25 g Japanese sea salad
4 tbsp flaxseeds, ground
2 tbsp nutritional yeast flakes
1 tbsp balsamic vinegar
2 tbsp sesame oil
2 tsp tamari

Pre-soak the sea salad for at least 20 mins; it needs a lot of water, at
least four times the quantity of water to sea salad. If you haven't got
pre-ground flaxseeds, grind them now. When the seaweed is ready,
drain, and add all the ingredients to the bowl. Give it a good toss, and
it's ready to serve. Keeps well in the fridge for up to a week.

Wild spaghetti western

Serves four
10 mins, 30 mins or more pre-soaking
No equipment needed

Wild foods are really good to include in your diet: they keep you in touch with your natural instincts, and are full of nutrition because they haven't been intensively farmed. Herbs are close to wild foods, especially ones that are organically grown.

Pre-soak the spaghetti for at least 30 minutes. Drain it when it's ready. Cube the avocado flesh and add to the seaweed. Chop the parsley as fine as you can, and add that too. Add the remaining ingredients and give it all a good mix together. Eat on the same day, or the maca starts to go bitter.

140 g (or 25 cm x 25 cm sheet) sea spaghetti
2 avocados
100 g or 1 large bunch parsley
2 tbsp maca
2 tbsp hemp protein
100 g or 1 cup sauerkraut

Alxxx is an angel

Serves two
15 mins
No equipment needed

It's not just me, everyone says it: Alxxx is an angel. I think it's something to do with the fact that when he was eighteen he got run over by a bus and was in a coma for two weeks. My theory is that he is a "walk-in", where the original soul leaves the body and a new soul comes in for fast-tracking; it doesn't have to go through the childhood stage, it comes straight in ready for action. So really, he's only eight, which explains completely his alluring combination of genuine innocence and wide-eyed wonder, and utter naughtiness and disregard for what the grown-ups say. This has got all his favourite things in.

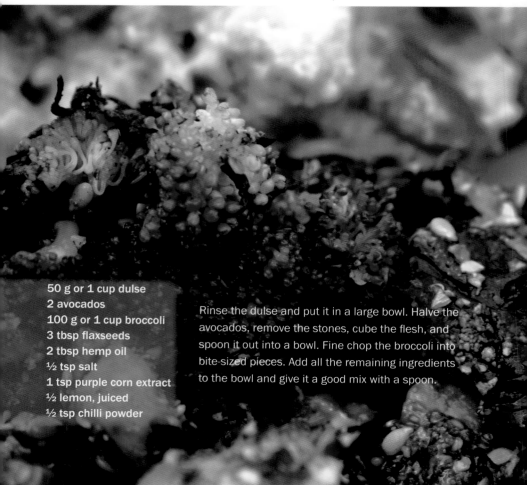

50 g or 1 cup dulse
2 avocados
100 g or 1 cup broccoli
3 tbsp flaxseeds
2 tbsp hemp oil
½ tsp salt
1 tsp purple corn extract
½ lemon, juiced
½ tsp chilli powder

Rinse the dulse and put it in a large bowl. Halve the avocados, remove the stones, cube the flesh, and spoon it out into a bowl. Fine chop the broccoli into bite-sized pieces. Add all the remaining ingredients to the bowl and give it a good mix with a spoon.

Ecstatic being salad

Serves two (main) or four (side dish)
No equipment needed
10 mins

This has everything in it – seaweed, hemp, cacao, maca, barleygrass, algae, gojis. Eat it every day for guaranteed enlightenment.

Tear the lettuce into bite-sized pieces. Rinse in a salad spinner for best results. Transfer to the salad bowl. Finely slice the cucumber and add to the salad bowl. Cube the avocado, and add. Dice the red onion as small as possible, and chop the coriander finely; add these too. Rinse the dulse and add that. Add the alfalfa sprouts, hemp seeds, Seagreens, cacao nibs, Sunseeds, goji berries and maca, and give it all a good toss so it's evenly mixed. Add the Greenvy and toss again, making sure the dressing is evenly coating the salad. Divide between the serving plates, and sprinkle with a little crystal manna for garnish. Bliss!

1 large purple oakleaf lettuce
½ cucumber
2 avocados
½ red onion
Small bunch coriander
25 g or ½ cup dulse
50 g or 1 cup alfalfa sprouts
2 tbsp hulled hemp seeds
2 tsp Seagreens
4 tbsp cacao nibs
50 g or ½ cup Sunseeds
2 tbsp goji berries
4 tbsp Greenvy (p98)
2 tbsp maca
1 tsp crystal manna

Sweet and spicy sunshine soup

Serves one
10 mins
Blender

Guaranteed to lift your spirits on a gloomy winter's day. This soup loves you and it wants you to be happy.

2 tomatoes
1 red pepper
2 carrots
2 sticks celery
1 avocado
1 red chilli pepper
1 clove garlic
1 lemon, juiced
100 g or 1 cup gojis & a few extra for garnish
¼ tsp crystal salt

Prepare your tomatoes, pepper, carrots, celery, avocado, chilli and garlic for the blender, removing any unwanted seeds and stems, and cutting into pieces small enough not to overload your machine. Put in the softer foods at the bottom, like tomatoes and pepper; carrots and celery are more likely to get stuck in the blades and jam it up. Add in the lemon juice and gojis, and blend for a few minutes until you have a thick gloop. You can warm this gently in a porringer, or just eat as it is. Garnish with a handful of gojis and a splattering of crystal salt.

Go go goji sauce

Serves two

15 mins

Blender

This is a superfood version of my signature dish, the eternally variable
Pasta Sauce recipe. The original recipe has cropped up in my books
Eat Smart, Eat Raw (Grub Street, 2002) and *Raw Living* (Grub Street, 2007). It's
also been published in magazine articles and workshops and has even appeared on
TV. It's a simple recipe that you can alter in an infinite multitude of ways to create
something different every time. Here it is chock full of gojis for a super fruity sauce.
Pour over veggies, steamed or raw, or add to wheat-free pasta, rice or quinoa.

Prepare your tomatoes, carrot, celery, onion and avocado for the
blender by removing unwanted seeds and stems, and cutting
into pieces to fit your blender without it complaining. Put
them all in, along with the remaining ingredients, and
give it all a good whiz for a few minutes until everything has amalgamated. Will keep in the fridge
for up to five days.

3 tomatoes
1 carrot
2 sticks celery
¼ red onion
1 avocado
50 g or 1 cup dulse
100 g or 1 cup goji berries
1 tbsp olive oil
1 tbsp apple cider vinegar
1 tsp tamari

Cacao'd up pasta sauce

Serves four

15 mins

Blender

Pasta sauce again, this time with chocolate. Inevitable, really. The presence of fats and sugars actually slows down the action of cacao in the body, so putting it into savoury dishes like this gives you a purer cacao buzz.

Pre-grind the cacao nibs in a grinder or high-speed blender. Grate the cacao butter, destalk and quarter the tomatoes, and add to the blender. Roughly chop the celery and carrots and pop them in too. Scoop out the avocado flesh with a spoon and in it goes. Next add the garlic, basil, vinegar, salt and dates. Blend for a few minutes (if the cacao butter goes a bit lumpy that's OK). Remove the sauce from the blender and put it in a porringer, or a pyrex bowl in a saucepan of hot water. Heat the water until the sauce is very slightly warmed and the butter is melted in. It's gorgeous to eat warm like this.

50 g or 1/3 cup cacao nibs
50 g or 1/3 cup cacao butter
5 tomatoes
4 sticks celery
2 carrots
1 avocado
2 cloves garlic
1 large bunch basil
1 tbsp apple cider vinegar
½ tsp salt
4 dates

Chocolate curry

Serves two
15 mins, 12 hrs pre-soaking
Blender

Cacao and spices are a natural combination, and
this green curry will have you wondering why we
don't traditionally put chocolate in savoury foods more often, it works so well.

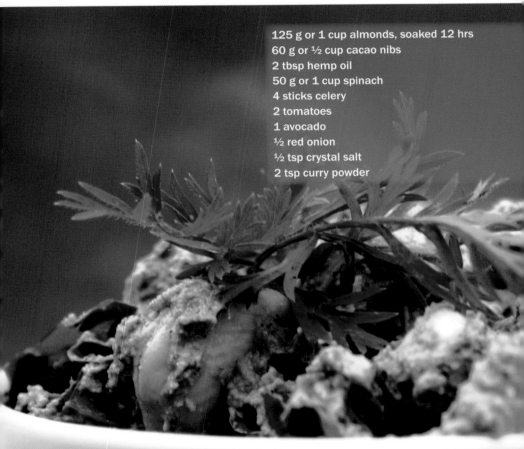

125 g or 1 cup almonds, soaked 12 hrs
60 g or ½ cup cacao nibs
2 tbsp hemp oil
50 g or 1 cup spinach
4 sticks celery
2 tomatoes
1 avocado
½ red onion
½ tsp crystal salt
2 tsp curry powder

Pre-soak the almonds overnight. When they're ready, drain and add to
the blender with the cacao nibs and hemp oil. Prepare your veg for the
blender by removing unwanted stems and seeds and chopping them into
small pieces. Put everything in, and give it a good whiz for a few minutes
until you have a thick puree. Serve as it is, or stir in your favourite vegetables, cooked or raw. Makes a great accompaniment to rice or quinoa.

Polly's perfect nori rolls

Makes 2 rolls

5 mins

No equipment needed

This is even better if you use fresh Percie de Sert pollen.

2 nori sheets
1 tbsp white almond butter
1 tsp white miso
1 tbsp flax oil
1 tbsp vinegar
2 tbsp bee pollen
½–1 avocado
2-4 broccoli florets
Handful or two baby leaf spinach
4 tbsp alfalfa sprouts

Lay out the nori sheets. In a small bowl, mix up the almond butter, miso, flax oil, vinegar and bee pollen with a teaspoon. Spread half of the mixture on each nori sheet, as a line along the middle lengthways. Halve the avocado and cube the flesh. Put half an avocado in each sheet, over the almond butter mix. Cut the broccoli into small bite-sized pieces and put half in each sheet. Next lay out the spinach and the alfalfa sprouts along the sheet, next to the avocado. With a little water on each sheet, wet the edges of the sheets' lengths – this helps it stick together when you roll it. Roll them up, rolling the edge nearest you over first, keeping it tight. Press the far edge down. If they're just for you, eat them as they are, like a baguette. If you're serving them to friends or family, you can cut each roll into four and stand them on end on a plate.

Rawlicious roll-ups

Makes four rolls

10 mins

No equipment needed

I find this the perfect dinner on the move: it fills me up and gives me energy to keep going with the next thing, happy and contented.

4 nori sheets
2 tbsp tahini
1 tbsp hemp oil
1 lemon, juiced
¼ tsp crystal salt
1 tsp crystal manna
½ tsp blue manna
1 large carrot
¼ cucumber
4 leaves lettuce
Alfalfa sprouts

Lay out your nori sheets. In a small bowl, mix up the tahini, flax oil, lemon juice, crystal salt, crystal manna, and blue manna with a spoon. Spread this mix in your nori rolls, half in each roll, in a wide strip lengthways across the middle of the roll. Cut the carrot and cucumber into thin matchsticks and lay these over the spread, half in each roll. Then tear the lettuce into small pieces and put two leaves in each roll. Finally lay the alfalfa alongside the vegetables. Wet the long edges of the nori sheet and roll tightly, starting with the end nearest you. Press the far edge down, and it's ready to eat. If you've made them for yourself, I would just eat them like that. For sharing, slice each roll into quarters with a sharp knife and serve standing up on a plate so you can see the spiral patterns inside the roll.

Magic multi-coloured kale

Serves two
20 mins
Blender

This makes an amazing purple, green and red salad with my three favourite salad ingredients: seaweed, greens and cacao.

Soak the Japanese sea salad in plenty of water – at least four times water to seaweed. While you're waiting, you can prepare the other parts of the dish. Take the kale and slice it into bite-sized slivers. Put it in the salad bowl with the cacao nibs, Seagreens and hemp seeds.

Remove the flesh from the avocado and put it in the blender – we are going to make an avocado pesto similar to the one in Raw Living. Put the vinegar, agave nectar, garlic and tamari in the blender. Remove excess stems from the basil and chop loosely. Quarter the tomato, pop it in the blender with the basil, and give it all a blend together so you get a thick cream with no bits of basil left.

When it's ready, transfer to the bowl with the kale in. By this time your sea salad should be ready; drain and add that to the bowl too. Give everything a good mix together, sprinkle with purple corn extract, and it's ready to eat.

25 g Clearspring Japanese sea vegetable salad
150 g or 3 cups purple kale
  (or green kale if you can't find it)
2 tbsp cacao nibs
1 tbsp Seagreens
2 tbsp hulled hemp seeds
1 avocado
1 tbsp apple cider vinegar
1 tsp agave nectar
1 clove garlic
1 tsp tamari
1 small bunch basil
1 tomato
1 tsp purple corn extract

Bold barleygrass stew

Serves one

10 mins

No equipment needed

This is a lovely warming winter dish – so simple to make, but very nurturing and satisfying.

½ red pepper
¼ head broccoli
1 stick celery
1 tbsp bean sprouts
1 tbsp corn kernels
2 tbsp dulse flakes
2 tbsp flaxseeds, ground
1 tbsp barleygrass
1 tsp miso
250 ml or 1 cup water, boiled
¼ tsp chilli or curry powder

Prepare your pepper, broccoli and celery by chopping them into small bite-sized chunks, a little bigger than the corn kernels. Grind the flaxseeds if they are not already pre-ground. Put the seeds in a bowl with the barleygrass, miso, and chilli or curry powder, and add the water a little at a time, stirring gently. Add more water if you want a thinner, less gloopy stew. Once you have added the water stir in the vegetables and all the remaining ingredients. Eat at once while it is warm. If you have a porringer, you can make this by putting all the ingredients in the pan, and heating it up that way.

Mermaid soup

Serves two
10 mins
Blender

I made this for the mermaids who live off Brighton beach. I think they would be proud. In fact, if you catch them at dusk, you'll see them dancing on the rocks.

1 cucumber
2 sticks celery
1 avocado
4 sheets nori
2 tbsp spirulina
½ tsp kelp
1 tsp cumin
250 ml water, boiled

Boil the water in your kettle. Chop the cucumber and celery into pieces to fit into your blender. Scoop the flesh out of the avocado and spoon that into the blender as well. Tear the nori sheets into quarters, and put them in along with the spirulina, kelp and cumin. Blend it all up to a cream, then pour the water in gradually as the blender is turning. Eat immediately.

Popeye loves you

He also loves Olive Oyl, which is why I used it in this recipe, but you can use hemp or flax oil if you prefer. Eat this for dinner and you'll be tearing up sails and lifting anchors like the man himself.

Make a dressing in a small bowl using the olive oil, tahini, maca and miso. Give it a good stir with a spoon until blended. In a larger bowl, add the spinach, sauerkraut and nori, pour the dressing over, and give it all a good mix. Left anything from a couple of hours to a couple of days, the spinach will wilt into the sauce just like it does when it's cooked.

2 tbsp olive oil
1 tbsp tahini
2 tbsp maca
1 tsp miso
2 tbsp nori flakes
100 g or 2 cups spinach
100 g or 1 cup sauerkraut

Rocket fuel soup

Serves two
15 mins
Blender

This has a spicy kick that will shift you up a gear. Makes a brilliant fast lunch. Heat it in the winter or have it chilled in the summer.

Prepare your tomatoes, pepper, celery, avocado, chilli and rocket for the blender by removing any seeds and stems and cutting them into manageable pieces. Rinse the dulse and put all your ingredients in the blender together, apart from one tablespoon cacao nibs. Whiz away for a few minutes until you have pureed everything until it's smooooooooth. Garnish with the remaining nibs.

2 tomatoes
2 peppers
4 sticks celery
1 avocado
1 red chilli pepper
100 g or 2 pressed cups rocket
50 g or 1 cup dulse
3 tbsp cacao nibs

Trenton's thai curry

Serves four
15 mins, 12 hrs pre-soaking
Blender

If I'm in a hurry, I like to cheat and use ready-made curry pastes. They're not raw, but the flavour is professional and authentic and it's so much quicker and easier than trying to track down oriental herbs. We use Geo-organics Thai Yellow curry paste in this one, and Meridian do some good vegan ones, but you can use whatever your favourite brand is.

60 g or ½ cup almonds, soaked 12 hrs
60 g or 1 cup sun-dried tomatoes, soaked 1 hr
100 g or 1 cup goji berries, soaked 1 hr
3 tomatoes
2 carrots
2 red peppers
4 sticks celery
½ red onion
1 bunch coriander
1 tbsp Thai curry paste
2 tbsp olive oil
1 lemon, juiced
100 g or 1 cup broccoli
100 g or 1 cup cauliflower
1 red pepper
50 g or 1 cup spinach
50 g or ½ cup cashew nuts

Pre-soak the almonds overnight. Soak the tomatoes and gojis one hour in advance. If you soak them separately, you can drink the goji soak water – I love it. Prepare your tomatoes, carrots, one of the red peppers, celery, onion and coriander for the blender by removing unwanted seeds and stems and chopping into small pieces so that they will not be too much hard work for your machine. Put the veg in the blender with the drained almonds, tomatoes and gojis, curry paste, olive oil and lemon juice. Whiz away for a few minutes until you have a thick puree. Remove from the blender and transfer to a large bowl. Prepare the broccoli, cauliflower and the remaining red pepper by dicing into small bite-sized pieces, removing unwanted seeds from the pepper. Add them into your sauce, along with the spinach and cashew nuts and give it all a really good stir, until the sauce is evenly coating the veg, and it's ready to go.

Twinkel's tasty chocolate cream

Serves two

Blender

15 mins

This sauce is lovely served warm, to release the aromatic oils of the cacao. Pour over a mix of your favourite vegetables like spinach, cauliflower, and steamed butternut squash. I've named it after Twinkel because it's pink and smells gorgeous, just like her.

100 g or ¾ cup cacao butter
2 large tomatoes
1 yellow pepper
4 sticks celery
100 g or ¾ cup hulled hemp seeds
1 clove garlic
1 tbsp agave nectar
½ tsp crystal salt

Start by melting the cacao butter. While it melts prepare your tomatoes, pepper and celery for the blender by removing extraneous stalks, stems and seeds and chopping them into pieces small enough not to worry your blender. Blend the vegetables up to a liquid. Then add the hemp, garlic, agave nectar, salt and melted butter and blend again.

crackers, breads and borgers
6.

Sorry, but you need a dehydrator for all the recipes in this section.

A dehydrator is like a raw-fooder's oven: it heats things at a very low temperature, so they are still technically considered raw as they are still enzymatically active, but foods get dried out enough to change them from soft doughs and batters to firm loaves and crispy crackers.

If you don't have a dehydrator you can still make most of these recipes in the oven, on the lowest setting, although they won't be raw that way.

Crackables

Makes 60 crackers
10 mins, 12 hrs pre-soaking, 18 hrs dehydrating
Blender, dehydrator

Flax crackers are a raw food staple: they make a cool snack because they go with anything, they add that extra crunch to any dinner, and they're infinitely variable. Simply soak flaxseeds in water, add any flavouring you choose, sweet or savoury, and dehydrate until crispy. Here we've put them with barleygrass to make the healthiest crackers on the block.

Soak the flaxseeds in the water for twelve hours. When ready, put the flax and water mixture in the blender. Peel and quarter the onion and put that in too with the barleygrass powder and lemon juice. Blend until you have a puree, with no seedy bits or onion chunks left. Spread over three dehydrator trays and dry for twelve hours. Score into 20 crackers to each tray, flip, and dry for a further six hours. Store them in an airtight container and they'll keep for two to three months.

250 g or 2 cups flaxseeds, pre-soaked 12 hrs
1 litre or 4 cups water
1 red onion
4 tbsp barleygrass
2 lemons, juiced

Fire wizard crackers

Makes 60 crackers
10 mins, 12 hrs pre-soaking,
18 hrs dehydrating
Dehydrator

Eat these and be burning up with magical powers! If you're a big chilli fan, you can slice up a red chilli pepper and add that into the mix too for extra fire.

Soak the flaxseeds in the water overnight. When ready, the seeds will have absorbed all the water and be one gloopy mass. Stir in the remaining ingredients by hand until the purple corn extract is evenly distributed in the flax and the result is an amazing purple colour. Spread over three dehydrator trays and dry for twelve hours. Score each tray into 20 crackers, four across by five down, and flip them over to dry through on the other side. Dry for a further six hours. Store them in an airtight container and they'll keep for up to eight weeks.

250 g or 2 cups flaxseeds, pre-soaked 12 hrs
750 ml or 3 cups water
1 tsp purple corn extract
1 tbsp curry powder
½ tsp crystal salt
2 lemons, juiced
100 g or 1 cup pollen

Green goddesses

These little babies go gorgeous topped with avocado and alfalfa sprouts. Lots of AmAzing foods begin with A – apples, artichokes, asparagus, angel delight….

Makes 25 biscuits
15 mins, 12 hrs pre-soaking,
dehydrating 18 hrs
Blender

Soak the pumpkin seeds overnight or for at least twelve hours. When they're ready, drain and add them to your blender with the dry flaxseed, Spirulina, tamari, and water. Prepare your onion by peeling and quartering it and add that too. Blend it all together for a couple of minutes until no seedy bits or onion chunks are visible. Stir in the Seagreens by hand. Spread over one dehydrator tray and dry for twelve hours. Then score into biscuits, five across by five down, and flip them over. Dry for another six hours. They make quite a moist biscuit, so store in the fridge and eat within two weeks or they will start going mouldy.

350 g or 2 cups pumpkin seeds, pre-soaked 12hrs
75 g or ½ cup flaxseeds
500 ml or 2 cups water
100 g or 1 cup spirulina
1 tbsp tamari
1 large red onion
1 tbsp Seagreens

Flaxtastic olive bread

Serves eight
10 mins, 18 hrs dehydrating
Blender, dehydrator

Kind of like raw ciabatta, you can add whatever you like to this gourmet bread — sun-dried tomatoes, poppy seeds, oregano, basil...

You need to use dry flaxseed for this to get the doughy effect. Pre-grind it first in a coffee grinder, spice mill or high-power blender. Peel your onion and cut it into at least eight pieces. Put the flax, onion, miso and water in the blender and quite quickly it should turn into a stiff dough. Stir in the olives and Seagreens by hand. Shape into a loaf about 5 cm (2 in) high; make it whatever shape you like — circles, hearts, and parallelograms are all good. Dehydrate for twelve hours, then flip over and dry for a further six hours on the other side. It'll still be soft and moist on the inside. Store in the fridge and eat within a week.

250 g or 1½ cups flax seed, ground
1 red onion
2 tsp miso
250 ml or 1 cup water
100 g or 1 cup pitted olives
1 tbsp Seagreens

Omega love loaf

Serves 12

15 mins, dehydrating 12 hrs

Blender, dehydrator

If you have a nut allergy or are catering for someone who has, you can still make a "nut loaf" using flaxseeds instead. Flaxseeds are a great binder and make a chewy, bread-like dough. You don't need to put suma in this if you don't have any, but it gives it that extra love factor.

Grind the flaxseeds. Peel the beetroot. Prepare your carrot, pepper, onion, celery and beetroot for the blender by removing unwanted seeds and stems, and chopping into small enough pieces. Use a high-power blender if you have one, or a food processor. Add all the veg first with 150 g (1½ cups) goji berries and the sun-dried tomatoes and blend for a few minutes until broken down. Add the flaxseeds, purple corn extract, suma, cumin and tamari, and process again into a dough. Remove the dough from the mixer and shape onto a dehydrator tray, about 5 cm (1 in) high. I like using a heart shape. Decorate with goji berries, a sprinkling of purple corn extract and hemp seeds, radiating out in a concentric pattern. Dehydrate for at least twelve hours. Keeps for a week in the fridge in an airtight container.

250 g or 2 cups flaxseeds
250 g or 3 carrots
2 red onions
250 g or 2 beetroot
150 g or 1½ cup goji berries
50 g or ½ cup sun dried tomatoes
1 tbsp purple corn extract
1 tbsp suma
1 tbsp cumin powder
1 tbsp tamari

Decoration:
2 tbsp goji berries
2 tbsp hulled hemp seeds
1 tsp purple corn extract

161

Love burgers

Makes 12 burgers
15 mins, 12 hrs pre-soaking, 12 hrs drying
Blender, dehydrator

Gojis and almonds are a good combination, gojis and garlic are a good combination, gojis and carrots are a good combination. These are good.

Pre-soak the almonds overnight, or for at least twelve hours. When they are ready, drain them. If you have a high-power blender you can make your burgers in that; if not, use a food processor. Grind your flaxseeds if you haven't already done so. Chop the tomatoes, carrot and coriander into small pieces to fit comfortably into your machine. Put everything in and blend to a thick paste. With your hands, shape into burgers about 1 cm high and 5 cm in diameter. Dry for about nine hours, then flip over and dry for three hours more. When they're crunchy on both sides, they're done. Will keep in an airtight container in the fridge for up to a week.

250 g or 2 cups almonds, soaked 12 hrs
50 g or 1/3 cup flaxseed, ground
2 tomatoes
1 carrot
Small bunch coriander
100 g or 1 cup gojis
2 cloves garlic
1 tbsp tamari

Choccoli biscuits

Choccoli = chocolate broccoli, two
of our favourite foods combined.

Makes 50 biscuits
10 mins, presoaking 12 hrs, drying 18 hrs
Blender, dehydrator

If you have purple kale or purple sprouting broccoli, you can make beautiful purple choccolis. These are gorgeous spread with some *Mayo maynot* (p109) and heaped with alfalfa sprouts.

Pre-soak the brazils and flaxseeds together in a bowl with the water overnight. When ready, pour the mixture into the blender. Chop the broccoli into small pieces and add that too. Peel and quarter the onion and pop that in with the nibs and vinegar. Blend to a thick puree so there are no bits of brazil or broccoli left. Spread evenly over two dehydrating trays. Dry for twelve hours, then score each sheet into squares, five across by five down. Flip the biscuits over and dry for another six hours. When they're ready, transfer   to an airtight container and they will keep for up to two weeks.

125 g or 1 cup brazils
75 g or ½ cup flax
500 ml or 2 cups water
250 g or 1 head broccoli
1 red onion
50 g or ½ cup cacao nibs
4 tbsp apple cider vinegar

Burger me

Serve with *Goji ketchup* (p102), *Cacaoslaw* (p123) and *Camu get me* (p285), and Micky Ds can go swivel.

Makes 10 burgers
15 mins, 18 hrs dehydrating
Blender, dehydrator

150g or 1 cup whole hemp seeds
2 tbsp flax seed, ground
150 g or 1 cup cacao nibs
1 red onion
Small bunch basil
2 carrots
4 sticks celery
4 dates
1 tbsp miso

Grind the hemp seeds, flax seeds and cacao nibs first in a coffee grinder or high-power blender. Then prepare all your veg by peeling and chopping into small pieces – onions, basil, carrot, celery and dates. Break them down in a high-power blender or your food processor. Then, in whichever machine you are using, put all your ingredients – seeds, nibs, veg and miso – together and mix for a few minutes until everything is amalgamated. Shape into patties about 1 cm high and 5 cm in diameter, and dry for twelve hours. Flip and dry for another six hours. Store in the fridge in an airtight container for up to a week.

Chiccolis

Serves six

15 mins, 2 hrs setting

No equipment needed

If I had to pick one genius idea out of this book, this might well be the one. Chilli-flavoured, chocolate-coated broccoli. Kind of on a Heston Blumenthal trip, combining unlikely ingredients into a dish that works shockingly brilliantly. Also works with celery (chocery), red pepper, olives (chocolives), even seaweed, whatever you fancy.

Start to make the chocolate by melting the cacao butter (p86). Put the cacao powder, mesquite, chilli and salt in a bowl, and mix them together with a spoon. Pour in the cacao butter and stir into a cream. Take your broccoli and snap off the individual florets, dipping them into the chocolate as thoroughly as you can. Lay them out on a large plate or tray and leave them in the fridge to set for a couple of hours. Serve as a snack or as an accompaniment to a salad for dinner.

110 g or 1 cup cacao butter
90 g or 1 cup cacao powder
75 g or ¾ cup mesquite
½ tsp chilli powder
½ tsp salt
250 g or 1 head broccoli

Puddings & breakfasts 7

Why are puddings and breakfasts in the same section you may be asking? Because with Raw Magic they're interchangeable!

Your puddings are so healthy you can eat them for breakfast, and your breakfasts are so good you'll want them for pudding.

Chocfast = chocolate for breakfast.

Pudfast = pudding for breakfast.

Really, when you start your day this way, every day, it's not long before every day becomes the best ever and you know you are living in heaven.

Purple mayhem

Breakfast madness. If you want to start your day in a tripped out purple haze, try this for size. Or you could end your day this way too. Or if you want real mayhem, have it at both ends of the day. Water of Life is an ionic mineral blend that contains all the trace minerals; it's not essential, but will help make this pudding love your body even more.

Put the chocolate powder, purple corn extract and mesquite in a small bowl. Pour in the tahini, agave nectar and water, and give it a good mix-up. Stir in the buckwheaties and mix again. Eat straight away: the buckwheat will go soft if you try and keep it more than a day or two.

1 tbsp choc powder
1 tsp purple corn extract
2 tbsp mesquite
1 tbsp tahini
1 tbsp agave nectar
2 tbsp water or Water of Life
100 g or 1 cup buckwheaties (see p86)

Goji mash-up

Serves two
5 mins
No equipment needed

We invented this at a service station one day when we didn't have access to a blender. We wanted pudding so we just threw together what we had and hey presto! As if by magic, a new favourite was born. Like *Pudding it right* (p180) but without the hassle of actually making it.

Scoop the avocado flesh out into a bowl with a spoon. Using a fork, mash it up as much as possible. Add the remaining ingredients into the bowl and mash again, making sure the agave nectar and tahini are evenly mixed in. Eat, and then get back in the car with some very good music to play loudly as you zoom down the motorway.

2 avocados
2 tsp agave nectar
2 tbsp tahini
4 tbsp goji berries
2 tbsp cacao nibs

Raw Magic heaven

Serves one
No equipment needed
5 mins

Alxxx and I invented this one day in the first shop back in 2006. It blew our trainers off. Since then I crave it if I'm feeling a little down or depleted. If this doesn't get you back into raw magic heaven, nothing will.

Make the pudding from the recipe on p180. Cut a Be the Change bar (or 40 g of your favourite raw chocolate) into small nibble sized pieces. Stir it into the pudding with half a bag of Raw Living's Magic Mix. If you haven't got Magic Mix you could just use goji berries and yacon root. Empty out the blue manna capsule into the pudding and stir it in. Eat and be transported into an instant whirlwind of over-ecsitement. God, we love it.

200 g Pudding it Right (p180)
1 x Be the Change bar
50 g Magic Mix
1 Blue Manna capsule

Perfect pollen

Serves two

5 mins

No equipment needed

How can I explain in words just how perfect this little combination is? It just does something to me that makes me feel that life is perfect again, that everything is just as it should be, and that good things always come to those who wait. On those days when I've got too much to do and no time to think, this is my life-saver.

100 g or 1 cup pollen
2 tbsp lucuma
1 tbsp tahini
1 tbsp flax oil
2 tbsp water or 1 tbsp water & 1 tbsp Water of Life
¼ tsp purple corn extract
½ tsp crystal manna
1 tsp chocolate powder
1 tsp honey

Mix everything together in a bowl with a spoon, and try not to eat it all at once unless you want to be flying round the flowers in ecstasy.

Green gloop

Serves four
10 mins
Blender

This recipe reminds me of the glorious Gela of www.rawreform.com. When we lived together we both had this affliction called Spirulina Mouth, which involved eating large quantities of spirulina, then smiling at someone and scaring them with our deep green teeth and lips. For some reason delivery men love to ring on the door just when you're eating spirulina.

Scoop the flesh out of the avocados and put it in the blender with the lucuma, spirulina, agave nectar and half the water. Put the blender on and slowly add the rest of the water until you have quite a thick pudding. Keeps in the fridge for up to a week. If you just can't help yourself, you can add 50 g (½ cup) chocolate powder and some extra agave nectar to taste, and turn this into a secretly chocolatey green gloop.

2 avocados
100 g or 1 cup lucuma
50 g or ½ cup spirulina
3 tbsp agave nectar
250 ml or 1 cup water

Goji porridge

Serves four
10 mins, 12 hours pre-soaking
Blender

Most oats sold commercially in the UK are steamed to stabilise them or they go rancid. At Raw Living we have sourced fresh raw oats which are packed specially for us. They only have a shelf-life of eight weeks but the difference in flavour is amazing. If you are into your raw foods it is worth getting hold of some. If you're using heat-treated oats, they are still a good source of fuel, and balancing for the blood sugar.

Soak the oats overnight. Soak the goji berries an hour in advance. Drink the soak water when they're ready – it's wondrous. Drain the oats and put them in the blender with the gojis, xylitol and water. Blend it up; it will seem really runny, but will thicken once heated. Put in a large pan and heat very gently over a low heat, keeping it under 118°F if possible (this is the temperature at which enzymes are destroyed and food stops technically being raw). Stir in the raisins and gojis. After about five minutes of stirring it should thicken nicely. Serve immediately. If you don't want to eat it all at once, the mixture will keep in the fridge for up to a week and you can just heat up as much as you need at a time.

Maca porridge

Serves four
10 mins, pre-soaking 12 hrs
Blender

Oats and maca are a really good combination. Both are stabilising to the blood sugar and give a long-lasting energy boost. Have this for breakfast and you'll feel calm, strong and capable of taking on anything the universe throws at you! If you're just making it for yourself you can blend up a batch and keep it in the fridge, heating up just what you need each day.

Soak the oats overnight in pure water. In the morning, drain and put in the blender with the maca, lucuma, xylitol, cinnamon and water. Blend it all up to a milk – it will be very runny still. Put in the pan and heat very gently over a low heat for five minutes. A porringer or double saucepan is ideal for this. Keep it under 118°F if you can, which is the temperature at which enzymes are killed and it stops being "officially" raw. Stir in the raisins and gojis. Eat immediately while warm.

250 g or 2 cups rolled oats,
soaked overnight
50 g or ½ cup goji berries, soaked 1 hr
2 tbsp xylitol
500 ml or 2 cups water
2 tbsp goji berries
2 tbsp raisins

250 g or 2 cups rolled oats, soaked overnight
4 tbsp maca
4 tbsp lucuma
2 tbsp xylitol
1 tbsp cinnamon
500 ml or 2 cups water
2 tbsp goji berries
2 tbsp raisins

77

Purple power pudding

Serves one
Blender
5 mins

Purple corn extract and cinnamon is an exceptionally tasty combination, and this pudding combines them with Etherium black to produce a treat that makes you feel empurpled and empowered.

Peel and pit the avocado. Put all the ingredients in the blender together and blend for a minute until smooth. Serve topped with blueberries, blackberries, or chopped figs – any purplicious fruit.

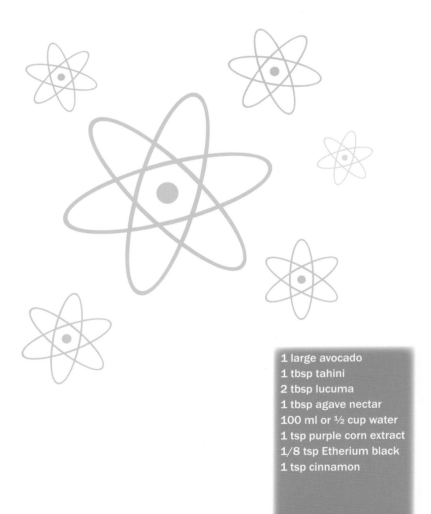

1 large avocado
1 tbsp tahini
2 tbsp lucuma
1 tbsp agave nectar
100 ml or ½ cup water
1 tsp purple corn extract
1/8 tsp Etherium black
1 tsp cinnamon

Pudding it right

Serves two
10 mins, 1 hr pre-soaking
Blender

Eat this and you will see no wrong in the world. This was our best-seller in the Raw Magic shop, after the chocolate. It's indulgent but also really refreshing and invigorating. The boys have it for breakfast as a treat. I have to credit Michelle Sugden, who was our fabulous cake maker at the time, for fine-tuning this recipe and getting it to this peak of sublimely mind-blowing perfection.

Soak the gojis in pure water one hour in advance. Drain, and drink the soak water as it's delicious. Remove the flesh from the avocados and put it in the blender. Add the coconut butter (you don't have to melt it first, it will break down in the blender), agave nectar, lucuma, camu, lemon juice and water. Give it all a whiz, then add the water slowly, keeping the blender running. When you have a thick dollopy pudding it's ready to serve. Sprinkle with gojis to decorate. Or try crumbling chocolate into it – have a look at *Raw Magic heaven* on p172.

100 g or 1 cup gojis, soaked 1 hr
2 avocados
2 tbsp coconut butter
2 tbsp agave nectar
2 tbsp lucuma
1 tbsp camu
½ lemon, juiced
500 ml or 2 cups water
1 tbsp gojis

Best ever breakfast cereal

Serves eight
10 mins
Dehydrator

The boys had this for breakfast every day for years. Sprouted buckwheat is a wonderful food, really grounding and calming but still light. You can vary it with any berry you like – try substituting mulberries for cranberries, or cacao nibs for bee pollen.

In a large mixing bowl, put the buckwheat, gojis, pollen, cranberries, and hemp. Give it all a good mix together. In a separate small bowl, pour the tahini, flax oil, agave nectar, lucuma, salt and probiotics. Stir it all up to a thick paste with a small spoon. Pour the paste over the buckwheat mix and give it a really good mix, making sure it's evenly coated. Store in an airtight container – it will keep in the fridge for up to a week. Don't add water to the mix or this will make the buckwheat go soggy.

200 g or 2 cups buckwheaties (see p86)
100 g or 1 cup goji berries
100 g or 1 cup bee pollen
100 g or 1 cup dried cranberries
100 g or ¾ cup hulled hemp seeds
2 tbsp tahini
2 tbsp flax oil
2 tbsp agave nectar
4 tbsp lucuma
1 tsp crystal salt
1 tbsp probiotics powder
  (optional – we use the Higher Nature brand)

Porringe

Porringe is our word for pink and orange together. Here we're using it to describe an orange porridge made with flaxseeds and pollen. You can buy pre-ground flaxseeds, which are really handy to have stored in the fridge, or you can grind them up yourself.

Boil the water. Grind the flaxseeds if you haven't already. Mix the flax-seeds, pollen, lucuma, agave nectar and flax oil together in a bowl. Gradually add the boiling water, stirring as you go, until you reach the desired consistency. Eat straight away while it's still warm. You can make purple porringe by adding half a teaspoon of purple corn extract, or chocolate porringe with 1 tbsp chocolate powder and a dash of extra agave.

250 ml or 1 cup water, just boiled
100 g or ¾ cup flaxseeds, ground
2 tbsp pollen
1 tbsp agave nectar
2 tbsp lucuma
1 tbsp flax oil

Chocolate chipper nicest icest cream

Serves four
5 mins, 20 mins freezing
Blender, ice cream maker

Who doesn't love chocolate ice cream? For a double chocolate treat, crumble a raw chocolate bar into the ice cream.

Blend up everything apart from the nibs. These are your choc-chips: stir them in afterwards, once everything's blended to a cream. Pour into the ice cream maker and proceed according to the manufacturer's instructions. If you don't have an ice cream maker you can pour it into a tupperware tub or pyrex bowl and leave it in the freezer for a couple of hours.

250 g or 2 cups hulled hemp seeds
75 g or ¾ cup raw chocolate powder
60 g or 1/3 cup xylitol
100 g or 1 cup mesquite
375 ml or 1½ cups water
100 g or 1 cup cacao nibs

Hempilicious ice cream

Serves four
5 mins, 20 mins freezing
Blender, ice cream maker

Ice cream makers are the best and easiest way I know of making raw ice cream, and hopefully you will have realised by now that raw ice cream is a pretty essential part of life. If you don't have one, you can just put the mix in the freezer for a couple of hours until it's frozen enough for you.

Put everything in the blender and blend to a cream. Pour into your ice cream maker and blend according to the manufacturer's instructions. Eat served with strawberries and goji berries on a hot summer's day for some hempilicious heavenliness.

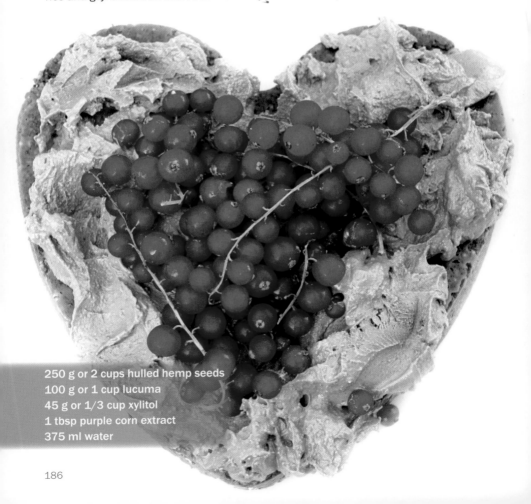

250 g or 2 cups hulled hemp seeds
100 g or 1 cup lucuma
45 g or 1/3 cup xylitol
1 tbsp purple corn extract
375 ml water

Call the police

Serves two
10 mins
Blender

I've made some of my best food when I've been heartbroken. As
Shazzie once said, "Chocolate or men? At least you get an answer out
of chocolate." There's no better way of reaffirming your status as a beautiful being
when you've been rejected by some silly person who doesn't know a good thing when
he sees it, than getting in the kitchen and creating yourself some gorgeousness. I
called this *Call the police* because it's so good it should be illegal. A bit like me.

Melt the cacao butter. Remove the
flesh from the avocados and put it
in the blender with the agave nectar,
mesquite, cacao powder, suma and
melted butter. Blend it all up and then
add the water gradually, keeping the
blender turning. Serve decorated
with cacao nibs and goji berries.

50 g or ½ cup cacao butter
2 avocados
1 tbsp agave nectar
100 g or 1 cup mesquite
50 g or ½ cup cacao powder
½ tsp suma
375 ml or 1½ cups water
1 tbsp cacao nibs
1 tbsp goji berries

Omegoji pudding

Serves four
10 mins, 1 hr pre-soaking
Blender

Oh my gojiness! Breakfast, lunch or dinner, this pudding will have you smiling for England, scraping out the bowl, and then dancing round the room in pure brain-food bliss.

Soak the goji berries in advance in pure water. Once they're ready, drink the soak water – it's delicious and nutritious. Put the hemp and flax in the blender and grind up to a powder. Then add in the soaked gojis, avocados, oils, xylitol and agave nectar and blend again to a cream. Keep blending, slowly adding the water. Once it's completely blended, transfer to two serving bowls and decorate with the remaining hemp seeds and goji berries.

100 g or 1 cup goji berries
50 g or ½ cup hulled hemp seeds
50 g or ½ cup flaxseed
2 avocados
1 tbsp hemp oil
1 tbsp flax oil
2 tbsp xylitol
2 tbsp agave nectar
250 ml or 1 cup water

Decoration
1 tbsp hulled hemp seeds
1 tbsp goji berries

Have I mentioned that finally, for the first time in human history, we truly can have our cake and eat it? That the world has never seen cakes the likes of these before?

So sublimely, divinely, orgasmically, beautifully inspired, they defy description?

So bursting with love on all levels, physical, emotional, mental and spiritual, that you will wonder how it has taken us so many millennia to get to this pinnacle of human existence?

Well, you will wonder for a minute, then you will take another bite of cake and not worry about anything much any more other than the next seed of bliss you can plant, the next gift of love you can give.

Tarts for the tart

Makes 12
30 mins, 2 hrs setting
Blender

One week I made these and couldn't stop eating them all week, they were all I wanted. Then I went round to Rochelle's house and she had made almost the exact same thing. Except I didn't have a name for mine, and she did, so here it is, the Tart's Tarts. They're a great thing to make and take away with you when you're travelling – they'll keep you going for days. If you're a maca fan you can substitute 50 g of the lucuma for maca. The result won't be as sweet, but it will be more energising.

Chocolate Topping:
100 g or 1 cup cacao butter
50 g or ½ cup chocolate powder
75 g or ¾ cup mesquite

First melt the cacao butter. Once liquid, remove from the heat and stir in the chocolate and mesquite. Pour over the short-bread and pop in the fridge for a couple of hours to set. Once hard, slice into twelve fingers, three across by four down. Keeps in the fridge for up to a week.

First melt the coconut butter. Grind the buckwheaties into flour in your blender, transfer to a mixing bowl and add the lucuma and xylitol. Mix well with your hands then add the melted butter and stir in with a spoon. Add the water and stir that in too. Press into a medium-sized rectangular tin. Leave out on the side while you make the chocolate layer.

Shortbread:
175 g or 1½ cups coconut butter
200 g or 2 cups buckwheaties (p86)
200 g or 2 cups lucuma
100 g or 2/3 cup xylitol
1 tbsp suma
250 ml or 1 cup water

Goji bucaroonis

Makes 16

10 mins, 3 days sprouting, 18 hrs dehydrating

Blender, dehydrator

Sprouted buckwheat is one of the best bases for making raw biscuits. Either sprout it and dehydrate it and grind it into flour, as in the *Tarts for the tart* recipe (p193), or sprout it and blend it up for a moister biscuit.

Sprout the buckwheat in advance. When it's ready, blend the buckwheat with the olive oil and agave nectar to a cream. Add the gojis and semi-blend them so you can still see bits of goji in the mix. Spread onto a dehydrator sheet and dry for twelve hours. Score into 16 biscuits, four rows of four, then flip over and dehydrate for a further six hours. Will keep in an airtight container for a few weeks.

250 g or 2 cups buckwheat, sprouted 2-3 days
60 ml or ½ cup olive oil
60 ml or ½ cup agave nectar
100 g or 1 cup gojis

Flaxjacks

These are so easy and so satisfying. Really good coated in chocolate too.

Makes 12
5 mins, 12 hrs dehydrating
Blender, dehydrator

150 g or 1¼ cups flaxseeds
150 g or 1¼ cups hulled hemp seeds
3 tbsp agave nectar
3 tbsp water

Grind the flax and hemp to a powder using your grinder or high-power blender. Then if you've got a high-power blender, add the agave nectar and water and blend again, otherwise transfer to a normal food processor and mix everything in there. The result should be a sticky mass. Press onto a dehydrating tray, about 1 cm (½ in) thick. Dry for six hours, then score into three rows by four columns. Flip over and dry for six hours more. Will keep for up to a week in an airtight container.

Whooshjaks

Whoosh is my favourite of our raw chocolate bars. The alchemical combination of cacao, maca and suma puts me right back where I want to be every time. Blissed but energized. Add oats into the mix too and you have a truly uplifting and nourishing treat.

Makes 20 biscuits
12 hrs pre-soaking, 10 mins, 18 hrs drying
Blender, dehydrator

Soak the oats overnight. Drain, and add to the blender with all the remaining ingredients except the coconut chips. Blend for a minute or two until it's pureed. Stir in the coconut chips, and spread on a dehydrator tray so it's about 1 cm (½ in) high. Dry for twelve hours, then score into biscuits four across by five down. Flip and dry for another six hours until firm. Will keep in an airtight tin for up to a week.

250 g or 2 cups oats, pre-soaked 12 hrs
100 g or 1 cup chocolate powder
75 g or ¾ cup maca
1 tbsp suma
100 g or 2/3 cup xylitol
60 ml or ½ cup olive oil
250 ml or 1 cup water
50 g or 1 cup coconut chips

Gojackajackas

OK, sometimes I get bored of giving you reasons to eat something. So give me one good reason not to eat these. Just one. See, you can't, can you? Nuff said.

Makes 20 biscuits
12 hrs pre-soaking, 10 mins,
18 hrs drying
Blender, dehydrator

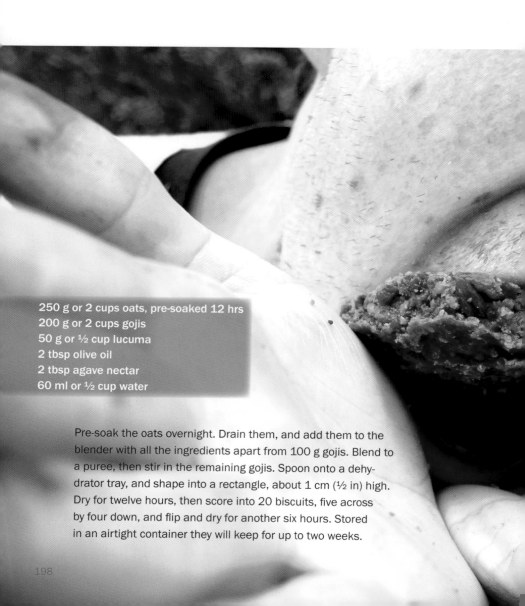

250 g or 2 cups oats, pre-soaked 12 hrs
200 g or 2 cups gojis
50 g or ½ cup lucuma
2 tbsp olive oil
2 tbsp agave nectar
60 ml or ½ cup water

Pre-soak the oats overnight. Drain them, and add them to the blender with all the ingredients apart from 100 g gojis. Blend to a puree, then stir in the remaining gojis. Spoon onto a dehydrator tray, and shape into a rectangle, about 1 cm (½ in) high. Dry for twelve hours, then score into 20 biscuits, five across by four down, and flip and dry for another six hours. Stored in an airtight container they will keep for up to two weeks.

Best ever brownies

These are based around the flapjack recipe from
my first book, *Eat Smart, Eat Raw*. I still use a
lot of recipes in that book on a daily basis, and
the flapjacks are one of them, but they have to be the Ace in the pack. They taste so
good, you'll be saying, "I can't believe they're not baked."

Makes 25
10 mins, 8-12 hrs pre-soaking,
18 hrs drying
Blender, dehydrator

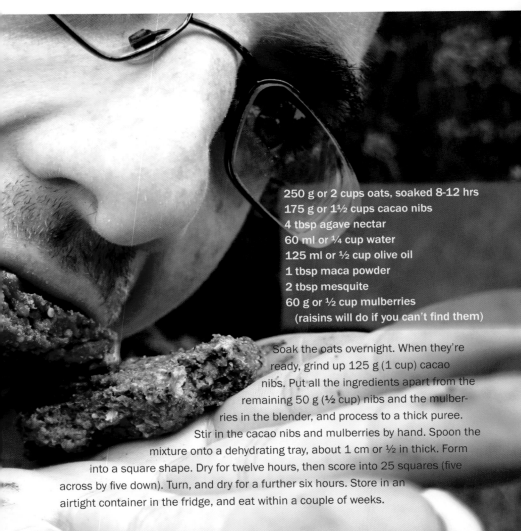

250 g or 2 cups oats, soaked 8-12 hrs
175 g or 1½ cups cacao nibs
4 tbsp agave nectar
60 ml or ¼ cup water
125 ml or ½ cup olive oil
1 tbsp maca powder
2 tbsp mesquite
60 g or ½ cup mulberries
(raisins will do if you can't find them)

Soak the oats overnight. When they're
ready, grind up 125 g (1 cup) cacao
nibs. Put all the ingredients apart from the
remaining 50 g (½ cup) nibs and the mulberries in the blender, and process to a thick puree.
Stir in the cacao nibs and mulberries by hand. Spoon the
mixture onto a dehydrating tray, about 1 cm or ½ in thick. Form
into a square shape. Dry for twelve hours, then score into 25 squares (five
across by five down). Turn, and dry for a further six hours. Store in an
airtight container in the fridge, and eat within a couple of weeks.

Chocolate crispy cakes

Makes 30 cakes
15 mins, 2 hrs setting
No equipment needed

If anything in this book is too good to be true, this is it. Buy some little paper cases from a cookshop to put them in, and when they're ready sit down in front a YouTube video of your favourite kids' TV programme to be transported into childhood nostalgic bliss. Then eat another one, and decide that being seven years old was pretty good, but actually here and now is the best it's ever been.

Start by melting the cacao butter. Put the mesquite, chocolate powder and xylitol in a bowl and stir in the melted butter. Quickly stir in the buckwheaties, raisins and hemp seeds – the mixture starts to set fast, so you have to be speedy, or get someone lovely to help you so you can do it in half the time. Take large spoons of the mixture and shape into balls with your hands, about 40 g in weight, or the size of a plum. Put them in little paper cases if you want, or just lay them on a tray. If you find the mixture sets faster than you can make balls, transfer it back into your melting device and remelt a little. Put the balls in the fridge to set, and an hour or two later they're ready. They keep for at least four weeks in the fridge.

220 g or 1¾ cups cacao butter
200 g or 2 cups mesquite
150 g or 1½ cups chocolate powder
45g or 1/3 cup xylitol
300 g or 3 cups buckwheaties (p86)
150 g or 1½ cups raisins
150 g or 1¼ cups hulled hemp seeds

Cor it's cornflakes cake

The lazy mum's chocolate crispy cake. For those who couldn't be bothered with paper cases, we used to get this version instead, pressed flat into a tin and cut into slices.

Serves eight
10 mins, 12 hrs pre-soaking,
12 hrs drying, 3 hrs setting
Dehydrator

Soak the flaxseed in the water overnight; it will swell and absorb it all. When it's ready, spread it over two dehydrator sheets and dry for about nine hours. Flip the sheets over and dry them for another three hours until fully crispy on both sides. When they're ready, it's time to make the chocolate.

250 g or 1½ cups flaxseed, pre-soaked 12 hrs
750 ml or 3 cups pure water
180 g or 1½ cups cacao butter
150 g or 1½ cups raw chocolate powder
150 g or 1½ cups mesquite
50 g or 1/3 cup xylitol

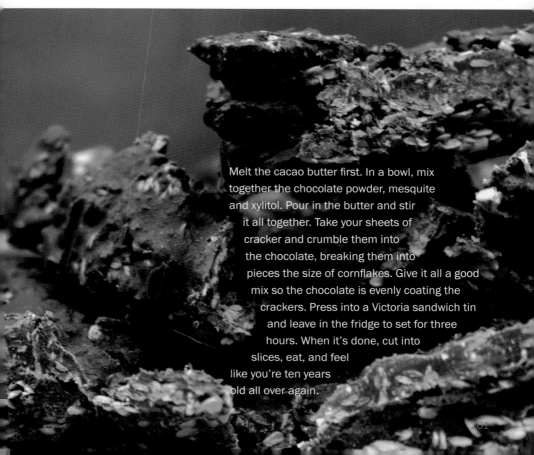

Melt the cacao butter first. In a bowl, mix together the chocolate powder, mesquite and xylitol. Pour in the butter and stir it all together. Take your sheets of cracker and crumble them into the chocolate, breaking them into pieces the size of cornflakes. Give it all a good mix so the chocolate is evenly coating the crackers. Press into a Victoria sandwich tin and leave in the fridge to set for three hours. When it's done, cut into slices, eat, and feel like you're ten years old all over again.

Kate's cinnamon chocolate bread

Serves six
5 mins, dehydrating 12 hrs
Blender, dehydrator

This is really filling, and so good if you split it in
half through the middle and spread it with yacon syrup and pumpkin seed butter
and eat it as a sandwich.

200 g or 1¾ cups flaxseeds
100 g or 2/3 cup cacao nibs
3 tbsp agave nectar
250 ml or 1 cup water
1 tsp cinnamon

Grind up the cacao nibs and flaxseeds; you can do
this together if you have a high-power blender, or
separately in a coffee grinder. Add the remaining
ingredients and blend again – the result will be a
very thick sticky mass. Spoon out and press onto
a dehydrator tray about 2 cm (1 in high) into a loaf
shape. Dehydrate for nine hours then flip over and dry on the other side for another
three hours. Stored in an airtight container, it will keep for a couple of weeks.

Hi-cake

Makes 8 large slices
30 mins, 3 hours setting time
Blender

Remember the Hi-bar? We started selling the Hi-bar in April 2005, the first raw chocolate bar to be sold in the UK. For some reason, we found it really hard to find good bar moulds, so for about six months we just had one single mould that the oompa loompas would press the chocolate into and turn out. We've got it framed on the wall of our kitchen now. This is the Hi-bar in a cake, made with cacao nibs and brazil nuts.

Grind up the nibs and nuts separately in a high-power blender or coffee grinder. Transfer to a mixing bowl with the lucuma and agave nectar. With your hands, mix all the ingredients so you have an even powder. Add the water gradually, kneading the mixture into a ball with your hands. It should end up as a fairly thick dough-like consistency. Press into a springform cake tin, and leave in the fridge to set for a few hours.

To make the icing, put the avocado flesh in the blender along with the chocolate powder, agave nectar and water. If you haven't got chocolate powder, you can substitute carob or mesquite. Blend until you have a thick cream.

Cake:
250 g or 2 cups cacao nibs
250 g or 2 cups brazil nuts
250 g or 2½ cups lucuma
6 tbsp agave nectar
150 ml or 2/3 cup water

Icing:
500 g or 2 avocados
30 g or 1/3 cup raw chocolate powder
2 tbsp agave nectar
60 ml or ¼ cup water

Decoration:
2 tbsp goji berries
2 tbsp dried cranberries

Once your cake is set, you can remove it from the cake tin and spoon the icing evenly over the top and the sides. Decorate with dried goji berries and cranberries sprinkled over the top. Uneaten cake can be stored in an airtight container in the fridge for up to two weeks (but only if no-one knows it's there).

Bee beautiful bread

Serves 16
10 mins, 12 hrs dehydrating
Grinder, dehydrator

If you want to be wise and wonderful, this is the stuff to have – slathered in *Love butter* (p249). Makes a bright and beautiful breakfast.

Grind the flaxseeds in a grinder or high-power blender. Transfer them to a mixing bowl with the lucuma, pollen, cacao and gojis, and mix it together with your hands. Pour in the honey and add the water gradually, kneading it into a ball as you go. Once you have a happy dough, shape into a loaf about 2 cm (1 in) high and place on a dehydrator tray. Dry for six hours, then flip over and dry for another six hours on the other side. Keeps for a couple of weeks in an airtight container.

300 g or 2 1/3 cups flaxseeds
150 g or 1 ½ cups lucuma
100 g or ½ cup honey
100 g or 1 cup pollen
50 g or ½ cup cacao nibs
100 g or 1 cup goji berries
300 ml or 1¼ cups water

Buzz cake

Serves 16
15 mins, 2 hrs setting
Blender

Iranian dried mulberries are becoming more popular and easy to find all the time. Try tracking them down in your local Eastern grocer or wholefood store. They're a very sweet, succulent berry which taste kind of like chewy honey. They go really well with pollen (see also p261).

Melt the butter first. If you have a high-power blender, you can put everything apart from the pollen in the blender together with the coconut butter and blend to a thick cream. If you don't have a high-power blender, grind the nibs, seeds, and dried fruit separately. Then add them to the blender with the purple corn extract and coconut butter. Once it's all thoroughly mixed, stir in the pollen by hand. Press into a cake tin or flan tin and leave to set in the fridge for 2–3 hours. Cut into squares: either 16 as a substantial pudding, or 32 for lots of little snacks. You can ice it with any of the creams and spreads in this book if you want to make it a bit more fancy.

200 g or 1 2/3 cups coconut butter
100 g or 1 cup raisins
100 g or 1 cup mulberries
100 g or 1 cup pumpkin seeds
100 g or 1 cup sunflower seeds
200 g or 1 2/3 cups cacao nibs
1 tbsp purple corn extract
100 g or 1 cup pollen

It just gets better biscuits

Makes 50

10 mins, 12 hrs pre-soaking,
12 hrs dehydrating, 4 hrs drying
Dehydrator

These are a bit of a faff to make, but so worth the effort. They look outstanding, with the purple cracker, red gojis, brown chocolate, white hemp and yellow pollen all complementing each other. They taste outrageously good and they're a fantastic way to have a balanced chocolate snack, with the flaxseeds giving them more density and bite, and all that algae and extra superfoods to get you really going.

Soak the flaxseeds in the water in a large bowl overnight, or for at least four hours, until the seeds have swelled and absorbed all the water. Soak the goji berries one hour in advance. With a spoon, stir in the gojis and purple corn extract until the corn is evenly mixed in and it has a beautiful purple hue. Spread over two and a half dehydrator trays – not too thin, or they will break when you take them out. About two-thirds of the way through drying, remove them and score each tray into crackers, four by five. Flip them over and let them dry through on the other side.

When they're ready, the next step is to make the chocolate. Melt the cacao butter, and when it's liquid remove the bowl from the pan and stir in the chocolate powder, mesquite and crystal manna. If you've got time, leave it to one side just for half an hour so it starts to thicken very slightly – this will make it easier to stick on the biscuits. Don't leave it too long or it will set too much. Dip the end of each cracker in the chocolate so that they are one-third to one-half covered.

Mix the hemp and pollen in a bowl, and take a teaspoon at a time and sprinkle them onto one side of the chocolate, quickly before the chocolate sets. They'll look like a Zoom lolly!

Lay them out on the dehydrator trays, being careful to keep them separate so they don't stick to one another (although they are pretty nice sandwiched together too), pollen side up. Unless you've got a lot of space, the best place to leave them to dry is probably in the dehydrator (don't turn it on!). They'll take about four hours to dry.

When they're done store in an airtight container – they'll keep for a few weeks.

Crackers:
25C g or 2 cups flaxseeds, pre-soaked 12 hrs
750 ml or 3 cups water
1 tbsp purple corn extract
100 g or 1 cup goji berries, pre-soaked 1 hr

Chocolate:
75 g or ¾ cup chocolate powder
125 g or 1 cup cacao butter
100 g or 1 cup mesquite
1 tbsp crystal manna

Topping:
2 tbsp hulled hemp seeds
2 tbsp bee pollen

The magic 23 cake

Serves 12
45 mins, 1 hr pre-soaking, 3 hrs setting
Blender

Cacao and gojis are astoundingly good together. I made this with Rochelle once, my co-collaborator on the Bullet Ride bar, and as it was the 23rd of the month we decided to name it *The magic 23 cake*. 23 is the cosmic trigger number: when you're tuned into the cosmic flow, when you're in the synchronicitous groove, you start seeing 23s all over the place. If you're not already in the Magic 23 place, this cake will put you there.

Pre-soak the gojis in pure water for an hour. You must drink the soak water or use it in the cake – don't throw it away, it's divine!

To make the crust, grind up the pecans in a high-power blender or coffee grinder. Transfer them to a mixing bowl and grind up the oats. Add them to the bowl along with the lucuma and toss it all together with your hands as if you were making normal pastry dough. Pour in the water gradually, kneading into a dough as you do so. When you have added just enough water to make it stick together in a ball, press it out into a large flan tin, lining the bottom and the sides with a crust about ½ cm thick. If you have any dough left over you can make it into little dough balls and eat it as it is, or make it into cookies and put it in the dehydrator.

To make the filling, melt the cacao butter first. Grind the nibs in a high-power blender or coffee grinder. Drain the gojis and put them in the blender. Scoop the flesh out of the avocados and put that in the blender too. Add in the nibs, butter, purple corn extract and agave nectar, and blend to a cream. Add the water gradually, as the blender is turning. After a minute, once you have a gorgeous smooth cream, spoon it out into your pastry case. Put in the fridge for three hours to set.

Stored in the fridge it will keep for up to a week.

Crust:
125 g or 1¼ cups pecans
125 g or 1¼ cups oats
125 g or 1¼ cups lucuma
125 ml or ½ cup water

Filling:
100 g or ¾ cup cacao butter
100 g or ¾ cup cacao nibs
150 g or 1½ cups goji berries, soaked 1 hour
500 g or 2 avocados
2 tsp purple corn extract
250 ml or 1 cup water
3 tbsp agave nectar

Right royal tart

Serves ten
1 hr, 2 hrs setting
Blender

Purple and gold together is a combination fit for royalty, to make you feel like the king or queen you really are. Eat this and reign supreme. Or better still, invite the Queen round for tea and offer her a slice.

To make the crust, grind the almonds and oats together in a high-power blender or coffee grinder until they become flour. Transfer them to a mixing bowl and add the lucuma and cinnamon. Rub it all together with your hands, like you're making usual pastry dough. When it's evenly mixed add the water gradually, mixing with your hands as you go, and kneading it into a dough.

When you have a ball it's ready to press into your large flan tin. Press it on the bottom and up the sides to make a shell. Don't make it too thick – if you have too much, reserve it and eat it as it is or make it into biscuits and dehydrate it. Store the crust in the fridge until you're ready to fill it.

To make the filling, remove the flesh from the avocados and put it straight in the blender. Add all the remaining ingredients and blend for a minute until you have a thick cream. Spoon it into the crust, and put it back in the fridge for a couple of hours to set.

Crust:
125 g or 1¼ cups cup lucuma
125 g or 1¼ cups rolled oats
125 g or 1¼ cups almonds
1 tbsp cinnamon
125 ml or ½ cup water

Filling:
750 g or 3 avocados
125 g or 1 cup
coconut butter
100 g or 1 cup
mesquite powder
1 tbsp purple corn extract
2 tsp Etherium gold
2 tbsp agave nectar
125 ml or ½ cup water

Superbliss tart

Serves ten
1 hr, 2 hrs setting
Blender

One day I went swimming in the sea and thought I was going to die because I went too far out and couldn't get back. I loved it. I came home and made up this.

Crust:
175 g or 1¾ cups almonds
175 g or 1¾ cups lucuma
4 tbsp agave nectar
1 tbsp cinnamon
125 ml or ½ cup water

To make the crust, grind up the almonds in a high-power blender. Transfer them to a mixing bowl and add the lucuma, stirring them together. Pour in the agave nectar and water, and mix by hand, kneading the dough into a ball. When it's firm, press into a large flan tin, and store in the fridge while you make the filling.

Filling:
75 g or 2/3 cup cacao butter
100 g or ¾ cup cacao nibs
750 g or 3 avocados
125 g mesquite
10 g suma
4 tbsp agave nectar
250 ml water

To make the filling, melt the cacao butter first. Grind the nibs in a high-power blender or coffee grinder. Slice open the avocados and spoon the flesh straight into your blender. Add the nibs, mesquite, suma, agave nectar, melted butter and water – everything, in fact. Blend for a few minutes until you have a light brown cream with no bits of nib left. Spoon into the crust and leave in the fridge to set for two hours.

Jesus loves you to gojiness tart

Serves ten
1 hr, 1 hr pre-soaking, 2 hrs setting
Blender

Jesus died for our sins, and this tart will do the same for you. Eat it and be redeemed.

Make sure you've pre-soaked your gojis for the filling. To make the crust, grind up the unsoaked gojis into a flour in a grinder or high-power blender. Transfer them to a mixing bowl and then grind up the oats. Put the oats in the bowl with the gojis and lucuma and mix the flours together with your hands. Add the water gradually, kneading the dough into a ball as you do. When you have one single mass, press it into your flan tin, lining the sides and the base about ½ cm (¼ in) thick. If you have any left over you can make little cookies with it and dehydrate it.

To make the filling, melt the cacao butter first. Scoop the flesh out of the avocados and put it in the blender. Add the mesquite, lemon juice, agave nectar, and gojis and blend to a cream. Keep blending and add the cacao butter gradually. Once you have a huge blob of orange smoothness, spoon it out into your flan tin. Pop in the fridge to set for a couple of hours. Will keep stored in the fridge for up to two weeks.

Crust:
125 g or 1¼ cups gojis
125 g or 1¼ cups oats
125 g or 1¼ cups lucuma
125 ml or ½ cup water

Filling:
200 g or 2 cups gojis, soaked 1 hr
100 g or ¾ cup cacao butter
750 g or 3 avocados
100 g or 1 cup mesquite
2 lemons, juiced
3 tbsp agave nectar
250 ml or 1 cup water

Matrix tart

Serves 12
1 hr, 3 hrs setting
Blender

OK, so this is like a deviant mincemeat tart. And when Zachary was only three years old he got The Matrix and mincemeat confused, as you do when you're three. But it actually fits because the apples and berries do make a kind of criss-cross matrix pattern. So see? Sometimes things that seem really silly at the time end up making perfect sense. Or sometimes the things that you thought made sense are actually nonsense.

Crust:
125 g or 1¼ cups gojis
60 g or ½ cup cacao powder
125 g or 1¼ cups almonds
60 g or ½ cup lucuma powder
125 ml or ½ cup water

Filling:
500 g or 1 lb apples
250 g or 2½ cups gojis
50 g or ½ cup cranberries
50 g or ½ cup barberries
50 g or ½ cup mulberries
100 g or 1 cup pine nuts
500 g or 2 avocados
2 tbsp flax oil
1 lemon, juiced
1 tbsp honey
1 tbsp cinnamon
1 tbsp psyllium

To make the crust, grind the gojis into flour in a high-power blender or grinder. Transfer them to a mixing bowl and add the cacao powder, almonds, and lucuma. Roll up your sleeves and mix it up with your hands. Add the water a little at a time, kneading as you go, so you end up with a firm ball of dough. Press it into your flan tin, lining the sides and the bottom with a layer about ½ cm (¼ in) thick. Any leftovers you can eat!

To make the filling, grate the apples and put them in a large mixing bowl with the gojis, cranberries, barberries, mulberries, and pine nuts. If you can't get hold of one or more of these berries, you can always substitute raisins or chopped dried apricots or dates. Put everything else in a blender: the avocado flesh, lemon juice, flax oil, honey, and cinnamon. Blend to a thick cream, then add the psyllium and give it another quick blitz. Spoon your avocado mix into your apple mix and stir it all together, making sure all your apple is coated in avocado. Spoon it into your flan tin and press it down. Pop in the fridge for a couple of hours to firm up. Serve with cream – *Maca'd up*, *Super hemp cream me* or *Angels are delighted*, whatever you like as long as it doesn't have cows in.

Blissberry tart

Serves 12
1 hr, 3 hrs setting
Blender

Berries and chocolate are a supersexy combination. Cherries are brilliant, if you can be bothered to sit and stone them. Blueberries are heavenly, if you can afford them. Or mix 'em up – strawberries and raspberries together are beautiful.

To make the crust, grind the oats to flour in a grinder or high-power blender. Transfer them to a mixing bowl and grind up the almonds. Put the almonds in the bowl with the oats and add the lucuma and chocolate powder. Give it all a good mix together with your clean hands. Add the water little by little, mixing with your hands and pressing the dough together to make a ball. Press into your flan tin, lining the sides and bottom with a layer about ½ cm (¼ in) thick. Any leftovers, roll into balls and eat. Put the case in the fridge while you make the filling.

To make the filling, melt the cacao butter first. Grind up the cacao nibs in a grinder or high-power blender. Remove any extraneous stems etc from the berries, and put them in the blender. Scoop the flesh out of the avocado and put that in too. Put the nibs and butter in, along with the mesquite, xylitol and purple corn extract, and give it all a good blend for a couple of minutes until you have a thick cream. Spoon it into your pastry case, and leave it in the fridge to set for a couple of hours more. Will keep in the fridge for up to one week.

Crust:
125 g or 1¼ cups oats
125 g or 1¼ cups almonds
60 g or ½ cup lucuma
60 g or ½ cup chocolate powder
125 ml or ½ cup water

Filling:
100 g or ¾ cup cacao butter
250 g or 2 cups cacao nibs
500 g or 4 cups strawberries, blueberries, cherries or raspberries
250 g or 1 avocado
100 g or 1 cup mesquite
75 g or ½ cup xylitol
1 tbsp purple corn extract

rassberry tart

Cacao crunch cake

Serves 12
1 hr, 3 hrs setting
Blender

So here's the true story of this cake. When I was 20 I had a bad trip on Brighton beach; when I was coming down the next day I ate a whole cake I had made, a vegan fridge cake with carob and broken biscuit crumbs and lots of sweetness. It tasted wonderful while I was eating it, but then I felt really sick, so I had some chips cos I needed something savoury, and then I felt even more sick and fat and not very happy. But the taste of that fridge cake haunted me, and when we moved to Brighton in 2005 I kept remembering it. I tried to recreate it, and this is the end result. A lot of people have said to me it's the best cake they've ever eaten. But if I hadn't had that bad trip, I'd never have come up with it 15 years later. Funny how things work, isn't it?

Melt the coconut butter to start. Grind up the nibs in a high-power blender or grinder. In a large mixing bowl stir together the nibs, lucuma, mesquite and purple corn extract. Once it's evenly mixed, add the Hi-trail. Hi-trail is our trail mix made with sprouted seeds, goji berries, raisins and cacao nibs, so if you don't have any Hi-trail, you can substitute with a combination of those ingredients. Then pour in your melted butter and mix it in to a sloppy goo. Pour it into a cake tin and leave to set in the fridge.

To make the icing, begin by melting the cacao butter. Once it's liquid, put it in the blender with the remaining ingredients. Blend to a cream, making sure the hemp seeds are fully blended in and the cream is not bitty. At this stage it will be quite runny. Spread on top of your cake, and it will set in 2-3 hours. When ready it should be firm, though still soft.

Crust:
220 g or 1¾ cups coconut butter
250 g or 2 cups cacao nibs
200 g or 2 cups lucuma
100 g or 1 cup mesquite
1 tbsp purple corn extract
250 g or 2½ cups Raw Living Hi-trail

Icing:
125 g or 1 cup cacao butter
125 g or 1 cup hulled hemp seeds
60 g or ½ cup mesquite powder
125 ml or ½ cup water
1 tsp purple corn extract

Cacao crunch cake

Quantum cake

"Kate makes Great Cakes which make you Late as you Ruminate," the wise proverb goes. Contemplate the Quantum Cake and create a quantum shift in your reality.

This is a sacred recipe personally given to me by the cacao gods. They have told me I am not allowed to divulge its magical properties to anyone or other than ecstatic things will happen to me. They have told me to tell you **it is the best cake eva** and if you want some you will have to buy it from our website. They have a wicked sense of humour, those cacao gods.

"That cake is the most exciting thing that's ever happened to me,"
K-Bomb from Trash Fashion

"Trash Fashion fully endorse this young lady's cakes. It is actually quantum. I've just taken a quantum leap. Bloody hell."
Trash Fashion www.trashfashion.co.uk

"I got a big piece of cake today. It arrived at 8am this morning and had been eaten by 8.30. Very nice it was too. Thanks very much for that burst of energy you sent to me today. I shall think of you at my moments of heightened pleasure... I'm addicted. I am proud of my addiction, and I don't mind if I get busted. There is nothing wrong with chocolate. Free it up. Peace, love and the good stuff."
Benjamin Zephaniah, Vegan poet, www.benjaminzephaniah.com

"Move over Mr Kipling, Miss Magic's cake is too good to be true ..."
Namalee, editor Super Super magazine, www.thesupersuper.com

"Your cake woz lovely and is definitely, beyond comparison, the most magickal."
Christopher Maguire, the UK's foremost wheatgrass grower

"So I sat down on Kate's infamous sofa and took a bite. 'This is the best raw cake I've ever had!' I delighted. Then I changed my mind and quickly corrected myself: 'This is the best cake I've ever had. Ever!' I was in total rapture as my eyelids closed and my mouth merged with the whole oneness of the great Universe. There has never been a better moment than when I took my first bite of Quantum Cake. Except when I took my next bite, because it does just get better."
Shazzie, Cambridge

"Quantum cake by Kate really is the best cake ever. It's truly the dessert of the next dimension, the goddess in a cake. Let it take you – if you are ready...

Bye bye Mr Bakewell, my mum was fond of your fancies.

Mr Kipling's ingredients, make no sense, if you want your cells to sing.

Sarah Lee, who is she, never seen her picture, is she on Myspace?

You stick to the pastry, if you wanna look pasty.

All that dairy is scary.

Well there's none of that in Kate's Magic – and about time!

It's a feast for your DNA, feel it sway, shimmer, get slimmer, indulge.

It's nice – have a slice..."

Chris Wood, Germany

Gratitude bread

Serves 10
10 mins, 12 hrs drying
Grinder, dehydrator

Gratitude is one of the most powerful emotions we can express, and severely under-rated in our culture where too much is never enough and we are conditioned to always look at what we can get out of a situation rather than what we can give. Take a moment in your day to eat some bread and count your blessings, and magically the more time you find in your life to be grateful, the more you find in your life to be grateful for.

250 g or 2 cups flaxseeds
100 g or 1 cup lucuma
3 tbsp agave nectar
1 tbsp purple corn extract
50 g or ½ cup goji berries
200 ml or ¾ cup water

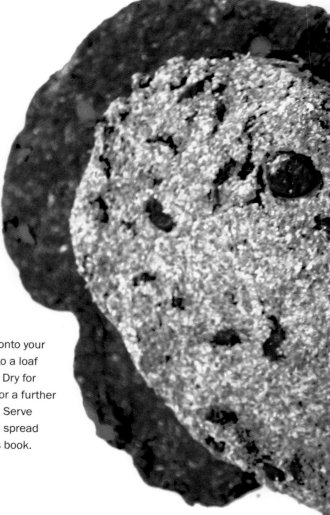

Grind the flaxseeds in a coffee grinder or high-power blender. Transfer them to a large mixing bowl, along with the lucuma, agave nectar, and purple corn extract, and give it all a good stir together with your hands. Add the goji berries and mix those in too. Add the water gradually, kneading as you go, so you end up with a big stiff ball of dough. Press this onto your dehydrator tray and flatten into a loaf shape about 2 cm (1 in) high. Dry for nine hours, then flip and dry for a further three hours on the other side. Serve sliced through the middle and spread with any of the spreads in this book.

Surrender to the confusion

Serves 10
10 mins, 12 hrs drying
Grinder, dehydrator

Sometimes life is just too hectic and confusing and impossible to make sense of. At times like these you need to make some of this bread, eat it, and feel that actually confusion can be quite helpful in making you surrender and let go and just relax and enjoy life a bit more.

225 g or 1¾ cups flaxseeds
100 g or 1 cup mesquite
50 g or ½ cup maca
3 tbsp agave nectar
100 g or 1 cup cranberries
150 ml or ½ cup water

Grind your flaxseeds in a high-power blender or coffee grinder. Transfer them to a mixing bowl with the mesquite, maca, agave nectar, and cranberries, and give it a good mix with your hands. Then pour in the water gradually, kneading it to a dough as you go. The result should be a ball which is fairly firm but pliable enough to shape into a loaf. Take a dehydrator tray and press your dough into a loaf shape (we like to make hearts), about 2 cm (1 in) high. Dry for six hours, then flip it over and dry for another six hours on the other side. Eat with any of the spreads in this book.

King Zachary's cake

Serves 12
1 hr, 3 hrs setting
Blender

What else would a little boy want for his cake on his fourth birthday but one made with berries and honey? And where else would he want to go but Legoland, and what else would he dress up as but a King? Truly, my children lead a dream life. Cake and Lego, I know how to treat them, like the Kings that they are.

Cake:
200 g or 1¾ cups cacao butter
200 g or 2 cups buckwheaties (p86)
100 g or 1 cup lucuma
50 g or ½ cup gojis
50 g or ½ cup mulberries
50 g or ½ cup barberries
50 g or ½ cup cranberries
100g or ½ cup honey
250 ml or 1 cup water

Icing:
250 g or 2 cups strawberries
1 banana
200 g or 1¾ cup coconut butter
50 g or 1/3 cup xylitol
4 tbsp agave nectar
175 g or 1¾ cup chocolate powder

Melt the cacao butter first. Grind the buckwheaties into flour in a grinder or high-power blender. In a mixing bowl, stir together the buckwheat flour and lucuma. Then add the gojis, mulberries, barberries and cranberries. If you can't get hold of one or more of these berries you can substitute with extra gojis or raisins. Stir them in, then pour in your honey and water, and blend to a runny dough using your hands or a spoon. Pop the dough into a spring-form cake tin and transfer to the fridge to start setting.

Start making the icing by melting the coconut butter. Prepare the strawberries and banana by chopping them into large bite-sized chunks. In a mixing bowl, pop in the chocolate powder, xylitol, and agave nectar, and give it a good mix. Stir in the butter, and when you've got a runny chocolate cream, stir in the bananas and strawberries. Pour this mix over the top of your cake so it forms a thick top layer about a quarter of the size of the cake mixture – it should just sit nicely on the top and fill the tin, not spill down the sides. After about three hours, when it's set, spring open your tin and slide the cake out.

Will keep for a week if the kids don't know where to find it.

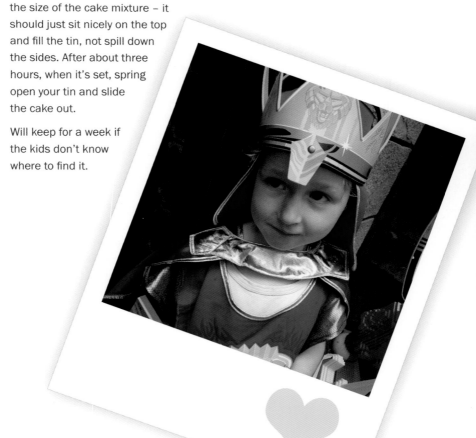

Cake mates

Serves 16
1 hr, 3 hrs setting
Blender

A cake mate is like a soul mate but better: someone with whom you can have your cake and eat it, someone whom you worship and who worships you back. I invented this in 2006 and since then I've yet to find anything to beat the sheer unbelievable wonder of it all. If you're not up for what is, quite honestly, a pretty tripped out cake, you can make it without all the extra added superfoods.

Base:
200 g or 1¾ cup coconut butter
100 g or 1 cup buckwheaties (p86)
100 g or 1 cup maca
100 g or 1 cup lucuma
1 tbsp suma
1 tsp Etherium gold
50 g or 1/3 cup xylitol

Chocolate layer:
240 g or 2 cups cacao butter
150 g or 1½ cups raw chocolate powder
200 g or 2 cups mesquite
2 tbsp crystal manna
1 tsp Etherium black

Topping:
750 g or 3 avocados
100 g or ¾ cup hulled hemp seeds
8 tbsp agave nectar
1 tbsp purple corn extract
1 tsp Etherium pink

Decoration:
2 tbsp goji berries
2 tbsp bee pollen
2 tbsp hulled hemp seeds

To make the base, first melt the coconut butter. Grind the buckwheaties into flour in your blender or grinder, and then transfer them to a mixing bowl. Add the maca, lucuma, suma, gold and xylitol and mix the powders together with your hands. Once they're well mixed, pour in the coconut butter, and stir it up with a spoon. Transfer immediately to a large flan dish and press down flat with a spoon. Pop in the fridge to help it set.

Next make the chocolate. Melt the cacao butter to start. In a mixing bowl, put your chocolate powder, mesquite, crystal manna and Etherium black and stir them together with a spoon. Once the butter's melted, stir that in too.

Remove the base from the fridge, and pour the chocolate layer on top. Put it back in the fridge. If you've got time, you may want to wait a couple of hours before making the next layer, to give the chocolate time to set.

To make the topping, remove the flesh from the avocados and transfer to the blender. Put in all the other ingredients and blend together to a thick purple cream.

Remove the cake from the fridge, and spoon the avocado mixture over the top. Decorate with the gojis, hemp and pollen in concentric circles. Any leftovers will keep in the fridge for up to a week, but only if you put an invisible protection spell over it so no-one can see it.

Cosmic cacao cake

Serves 10
1 hr, 3 hrs setting
Blender

This was our most popular cake in the Raw Magic shop. You can vary it with any nut or seed to replace the sesame. If you can't be bothered to make it yourself, we also sell this one online in lots of different incarnations.

Icing:
500g or 2 avocados
30 g or ¼ cup chocolate powder
2 tbsp agave nectar
1 tbsp suma
2 tbsp bee pollen
2 tbsp hulled hemp seeds

Cake:
250 g or 2 cups sesame seeds
250 g or 2 cups cacao nibs
200 g or 2 cups lucuma
90 g or 2/3 cup xylitol
250 ml or 1 cup water

Grind the sesame seeds up in a high-power blender or grinder. Transfer them to a large mixing bowl. Grind the nibs up in the same way and put them in the bowl too. Add the lucuma and xylitol and give it all a good stir so it's evenly mixed. Pour in the water and stir it in so you have a thick cookie mixture. Spoon it into a cake tin and pop in the fridge to set for three hours.

Once it's ready, you can make your icing. Peel the avocados, spoon out the flesh and put them in the blender. Add the chocolate powder, agave nectar and suma and blend it all together to a cream. Spoon over the top and sides of the cake so it covers the whole cake evenly. Decorate the top with the bee pollen and hemp seeds.

Macajackas

Makes 20 biscuits
12 hrs pre-soaking, 10 mins, 18 hrs drying
Blender, dehydrator

I love maca and oats together – they really complement each other. Calming and nourishing, you feel like you can conquer the world, but actually you don't need to because everything's perfect.

Soak the oats overnight. Drain, and put in the blender with all the other ingredients except the raisins. Blend to a puree then stir in the raisins by hand. Spoon out onto a dehydrator tray, and spread into a square about 1 cm (½ in) high. Dry for twelve hours, then score into 20 biscuits, five across by four down. Dry for another six hours. Will keep in an airtight container for up to a week.

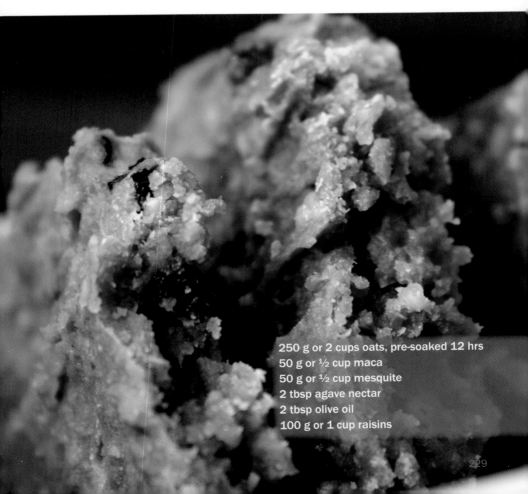

250 g or 2 cups oats, pre-soaked 12 hrs
50 g or ½ cup maca
50 g or ½ cup mesquite
2 tbsp agave nectar
2 tbsp olive oil
100 g or 1 cup raisins

Believe it or not, sometimes you want a sweet snack that isn't chocolate. Sometimes chocolate just won't cut the custard, and that's where these little babies come in.

We've got lots of fudge, some trail mixes, and some creams for spreading on crackers, using as cake icings, pouring over fruit, or just over your best friend. In fact, pour them over anybody you take a fancy to, and if they're not your best friend already, then they soon will be.

Fudging awesome

Everyone loves gojis, and everyone loves goji fudge. And be warned, everyone eats too much of this when they first try it.

Makes 16 squares
10 mins, 2-3 hrs setting
Blender

Melt the coconut butter first. Pour it in a high-power blender with the gojis and agave nectar. Blend for a few minutes. They won't form a cream, but the gojis will break down into a mass. It's tricky to get it right – if you blend too long, the oil in the gojis will start to separate; but if you don't blend long enough your end result will not be smooth. Add the mesquite and lucuma and blend again – this time it should make a cream. Pour into a small tray and leave it to set in the fridge for 2-3 hours. Once it's hard, cut into 16 squares.

150 g or 1¼ cups coconut butter
100 g or 1 cup gojis
3 tbsp agave nectar
75 g or ¾ cup mesquite
75 g or ¾ cup lucuma

Crystal omega fudge

Makes 30 squares
10 mins, 2 hrs setting
Blender

There are a few different types of omega butter on the
market – we usually use Carley's Mixed Seed Butter or
Detox your World Hemp Seed Butter, but any nut butter made from pumpkin,
hemp, sesame, or a combination of omega-rich seeds will work.

150 g or 1¼ cups coconut butter
150 g or ¾ cup omega butter
100 g or 1 cup mesquite
100 g or 1 cup maca
3 tbsp agave nectar
2 tbsp crystal manna

Melt the coconut butter first. In a blender,
blend the melted coconut with the omega
butter to a liquid. Then add the mesquite,
maca and agave nectar and blend again. Stir
in the crystal manna and pour into a large
tray. Set in the fridge for 2-3 hours. Turn out
and cut into cubes, five across by six down.

Golden goji love

Makes 25 sqares
10 mins, 2 hrs setting
Blender

We use the heart-shaped silicon ice-cube trays for these – they are quite easy to find in cookshops and supermarkets if you haven't got professional heart moulds. Failing that, you can just pour the mix into the tray and cut into cubes.

Start by melting the cacao butter. Put the goji berries in a high-power blender or grinder, and grind to a powder. It doesn't have to be too fine, just as long as there are no whole berries left. Add the agave nectar and melted butter and blend again to a liquid. Then add the lucuma and gold and briefly blend one more time. Do not over-blend or the oil from the gojis will start to separate. Pour into moulds and leave for at least two hours to set. When they're ready, pop them out, and remember, these are for SHARING.

150 g or 1¼ cups cacao butter
100g or 1 cup goji berries
3 tbsp agave nectar
100 g or 1 cup lucuma
1 tsp Etherium gold

All that glitters is not green

Makes 25 squares
10 mins, 3 hrs setting
No equipment needed

OK, I admit it, it's hard to make spirulina taste nice. A few people like it, but most people find it pretty hard to stomach. I've done my best here to cram algae into a sweet bar that tastes so yummy you'll keep eating it.

150 g or 1½ cups cacao butter
75 g or ¾ cup spirulina
50 g or ½ cup mesquite
50 g or ½ cup lucuma
1 tbsp agave nectar
1 tbsp crystal manna

Melt the cacao butter first. Once it's liquid, transfer to a mixing bowl and stir in all the other ingredients, leaving ½ tbsp crystal manna aside. Give it all a good stir and pour into a medium-sized tray. Sprinkle on the remaining tablespoon of crystal manna, pressing it gently into the fudge. Leave in the fridge to set for three hours. When it's ready, turn out carefully, trying not to lose any of the crystal manna from the top. Cut into cubes, five by five.

Macaculous fudge

Cacao butter and lucuma is such a great combination in sweets. As this book goes to press I'm working on a raw version of custard creams which takes advantage of this very partnership to make the most delicious accompaniment to a cup of tea I have ever experienced.

Makes 25 squares
10 mins, 3 hours setting
Blender

100 g or ¾ cup cacao butter
125 g or 1 cup hulled hemp seeds
100 g or 1 cup maca
50 g or ½ cup lucuma
3 tbsp agave nectar
1 tsp Aulterra

Melt the butter. Mash the hemp seeds to a paste in a blender or food grinder. Add the melted butter and blend again so you have a runny cream. Add the remaining ingredients and blend one more time. Press into a tray and leave in the fridge for three hours to set – you should have a solid but soft fudge. When it's ready, turn out and cut into squares, five by five. Keeps for up to a week in the fridge.

Fudge me

We used to sell a lot of this in the Raw Magic shop. It's very filling, grounding and energising without being over-stimulating like chocolate sometimes can be.

Makes 16 squares
15 mins, 2 hrs setting
Blender

220 g or 1¾ cups hulled hemp seeds
50 g or ½ cup mesquite powder
2 tbsp agave nectar
1 tsp suma

Grind up the hemp seeds in a high-power blender or grinder. If you're using a high-power blender add the mesquite and agave nectar, otherwise transfer to a food processor and blend again. When you have a sticky mass, scrape it out with a spoon and press into a small tray. Leave it in the fridge to set for two hours. When it's ready, cut into cubes, four across by four down. Keeps for up to a week in the fridge.

Caramaca

Makes 16 squares
10 mins, 3 hrs setting
No equipment needed

This was one of the first sweets we sold, originally known as Maca Bar. It's super-strengthening and very moreish, but unfortunately it doesn't keep well so we had to stop making it. Maca tastes a bit like sick when it goes rancid, which isn't what you want from a sweet treat really, is it?

100 g or 1 cup maca
100 g or 1 cup mesquite
150 g or 1¼ cup coconut butter
1 tbsp vanilla powder or 1 tbsp vanilla essence

Melt the coconut butter first. When it's liquid, transfer to a mixing bowl and stir in the mesquite, maca and vanilla. Pour into a small tray and leave in the fridge to set for 2-3 hours. When it's ready, turn out and cut into cubes, four across by four down. Keeps in the fridge for up to one week.

It's the buzzness

Everyone loves this fudge, it's a perfect pick-me-up.
Bee pollen and purple corn extract are a winning team:
purple keeps you focused while the pollen keeps you moving.

Makes 25 squares
10 mins, 3 hours setting
No equipment needed

150 g or 1¼ cups coconut butter
150 g or 1½ cups bee pollen
150 g or 1½ cups lucuma
½ tsp crystal salt
1 tsp purple corn extract

Melt the butter first. Once it's liquid, stir all
the ingredients together in a bowl and pour
into a tray to set. Leave in the fridge for
three hours, by which time it should be hard.
Turn out and cut into cubes, five by five.

Camu believe it

This is a gorgeously gentle fudge, for when you actually don't feel like being energised, tripped out or shaken up much at all. Better make a double batch if you want to eat any yourself – this one disappears faster than you can say, "I only made that yesterday."

Melt both butters together. Mash the hemp seeds up in a blender or grinder. Then blend them up with the melted butters. Add the remaining ingredients to the blender and blend one more time. Pour into a medium sized tray and leave in the fridge to set for three hours. When it's hard, turn out and cut into cubes, five across by five down.

- 100 g or ¾ cup cacao butter
- 100 g or ¾ cup coconut butter
- 100 g or ¾ cup hulled hemp seeds
- 3 tbsp agave nectar
- 100 g or 1 cup mesquite
- 100 g or 1 cup lucuma
- 2 tbsp camu
- 1 tbsp purple corn extract

Mulberry mud

Makes 20 squares
15 mins, 3 hrs setting
Blender

Mud, mud, glorious mud, there's nothing quite like it for cooling the blood. I can't actually say for sure that this fudge will cool your blood, but it will do something to your body that could make you dance around the kitchen in a pleasant sort of muddy mulberry madness.

Start off by melting the cacao butter. Blend the mulberries to a mash in the blender. Add the melted butter and blend again to a liquid. Add the mesquite, Etherium red, and suma and blend one more time until you have a smooth cream. Pour into a medium-sized tray and leave to set in the fridge for three hours. When it's ready, turn it out and cut into cubes, five across by four down, 20 all together. Will keep stored in the fridge for a couple of weeks.

150 g or 1¼ cups cacao butter
200 g or 2 cups mulberries
100 g or 1 cup mesquite
1 tsp Etherium red
1 tbsp suma

Super hemp cream me

This is gorgeous as a dip for fruit and perfect as an icing for cakes – or spread it on bread for a teatime snack.

Put all the ingredients in the blender together and blend for a couple of minutes until you have a thick cream. Keeps in the fridge for up to a week. It will thicken when stored, so you may want to add a little extra water.

250 g or 2 cups hulled hemp seeds
125 g or 1¼ cups lucuma
90 g or 1 cup xylitol
1 vanilla pod or 1 tbsp vanilla powder
250 ml or 1 cup water

Matchmake me

Makes one jar
10 mins
Blender

Cheeky and minty. As you stir this visualise your perfect chocolate boyfriend or girlfriend and then when you meet them you
will know it was all down to eating this spread on bread at 2.30 every day for after-
noon tea, and you can write and thank me, and send me pictures showing how
beautiful you look together.

100 g or ¾ cup coconut butter
100 g or ¾ cup hemp seeds
50 g or ½ cup xylitol
5 drops peppermint oil
60 ml or ¼ cup water

Melt the coconut butter first. Mash the hemp
seeds in the blender, then add the melted butter
and blend again. Add the xylitol and peppermint
oil and keep the blender turning while you add
the water gradually. Once it's done, you can eat
it like this as a runny cream over fruit, or leave
it in the fridge to harden into more of a spread.

Barleypear

Serves four
5 mins, 12 hrs drying
Blender, dehydrator

This is a brilliant way to get the alkalising greens into kids – or yourself. They make perfect snacks to put into packed lunches. You can also make the same recipe with spirulina and apple.

Remove the stems from the pears and slice them into pieces to fit comfortably into your blender, removing cores and seeds. Put them in the blender with the barleygrass and whiz for a few minutes until there are no lumps of pear left. Spread over drying sheets and dry for twelve hours. When they're leathery and there are no moist bits left, remove them and tear into strips. Store in an airtight container – they will keep for several weeks.

500 g or 2 large pears
1 tbsp barleygrass powder

245

Maca'd up

Serves four

5 mins

No equipment needed

This is so beautifully quick and simple to make, goes lovely on bread, and is a nice easy way to make sure you get your maca in you.

Spoon it all into a bowl apart from the water. With a small spoon, give it a good stir. The maca is very absorbent and your mixture will go very dry and stiff. (You can just eat it like this if you're feeling piggy! Or roll it into walnut-sized balls to make little sweeties.) Add the water, a table-spoon at a time, until you reach the desired consistency – runny like tahini. The end result should be sweet, rich, creamy, and utterly irresistible.

4 tbsp maca powder
4 tbsp tahini
4 tbsp agave nectar
4 tbsp hemp oil
250 ml or 1 cup pure water

Purple love cream

Have your way with this cream. Spread it on bread, use it as a fondant centre in chocolate making, dip strawberries in it, or cover someone you love in it and lick it off. Yum…

Mix everything together in a bowl with a spoon to form a paste. Store in the fridge. Keeps well.

3 tbsp agave nectar
50 g or ¼ cup tahini
2 tsp purple corn extract
2 tsp liquid maca extract (maca tincture)
5 drops rose essential oil

Right said Fred spread

Serves six

5 mins

No equipment needed

Remember them? If this spread could sing it would go, "I'm too sexy, I'm too sexy for this recipe book". Deadly simple, deadly effective, deadly delicious, spread this on anything if you are ready to die and go to heaven.

3 tbsp raw chocolate powder
2 tbsp white almond butter
2 tbsp flax oil
2 tbsp raw honey
1 tsp suma

Put everything in a large bowl and mix with a spoon. Store in the fridge, it will keep for a couple of weeks.

Love butter

No ifs, no buts, just love.

Put everything in the blender apart from the water. Mash up the hemp seeds a bit then gradually add the water, keeping the blender running as you go. Give it a minute or two, then it's ready. Keeps in the fridge, although keep it away from things that go off easily, this butter is HOT.

250 g or 2 cups hulled hemp seeds
75 g or ¾ cup chocolate powder
50 g or ½ cup maca
4 tbsp raw honey
1 tsp white miso
2 tbsp hemp oil
350 ml or 1½ cups water

Space dust

Serves four

5 mins

No equipment needed

This makes a joyous sprinkle for cereal, yoghurt, cake toppings, salad – anything that could do with a little extra joy, in short. It kind of tingles in your mouth and brightens up your life.

4 tbsp bee pollen
4 tbsp hulled hemp seeds
4 tbsp cacao nibs
2 tbsp raisins

Mix! You can even just eat it straight as it is – it's perfect for when you're on the go and don't have time to eat anything.

Super super trail

Another super-easy, super-energising trail mix to add to anything and everything and spread a little super-superness.

Serves four
5 mins
No equipment needed

And...
mix!
And...
eat!

50 g or ½ cup gojis
25 g or ½ cup coconut chips
50 g or ½ cup cacao nibs
25 g or ¼ cup raisins
25 g or ¼ cup bee pollen

Angels are delighted

Serves four
15 mins
Blender

This cream will transport even the most depraved and sinful of you to heaven immediately. If I were Queen, I would put it on the NHS and then we could all live in fluffy pink cloudland every day.

Remove the flesh from the avocado and scoop it into the blender. Add the hemp seeds, camu and xylitol and blend to a cream. With the blender running, add the water gradually. Store in the fridge – it will keep for up to a week.

1 avocado
100 g or ¾ cup hulled hemp seeds
2 tbsp camu
75 g or ¾ cup xylitol
250 ml or 1 cup water

Angels are delighted

253

Ok, well you know what? I think this book is worth the cover price for these chocolate recipes alone.

I can think of only one other person in the country who may have as much raw chocolate-making experience as me (Mz Dazzle). We were fortunate to be among the first people in the UK to be introduced to the wonders of raw chocolate, and since then my kitchen and my shop have become famous for the alchemical wonders I produce. It has become a staple part of our diet, and the many people who live and pass through our household eat it on a daily basis.

How many mothers try and make sure their children eat their chocolate every day?!

I always lace it with superfoods: so as well as the extraordinary nutritional content of the cacao they get extras like algae, bee pollen, maca and goji berries. The Etheriums also work really well in chocolate. Where I have included Etheriums in the recipes, you can always omit them if they're not available – it won't affect the taste. And you can also add them to any recipe if you feel drawn to do so.

So here are a few of my favourite recipes, born out of testing over and over again what works (it's a hard job, but someone has to be a kitchen cacao slave, making the most wondrous food ever day after day after day). And remember, chocolate-making is therapy, and chocolate-making is fun! So use your imagination, be intuitive, and let yourself go wild in the kitchen creating your own alchemical cacao creations.

I always put a pinch of Himalayan crystal salt in my chocolate recipes – it improves the flavour and aids mineral absorption. Just quarter of a teaspoon is enough in a batch of chocolate. I haven't mentioned it in the recipes, but if you have some to hand it's a good idea to include it.

For a tray to pour it into, I either use a small baking tray or a large Tupperware container. If you want to make chocolate as a gift, ice cube trays make good little moulds, and you can get all sorts of designs now – hearts are popular. The silicon baking moulds you find in cook shops also work well.

One last tip, courtesy of Madame Von Rockstar – if you're using a blender, when you've scraped the chocolate out of the blender jug pour in a cup of pure boiling water and give it another blend. This will help clean the jug, but better than that the resulting liquid is gorgeous as a creamy hot chocolate drink.

Wherever possible I measure the ingredients for chocolate recipes using scales – it's much more accurate. For most raw cuisine 10 g here or there doesn't generally make much difference, but chocolate making is a bit more of a science and it's best to be as spot on as you can be.

Most chocolates keep in the fridge for up to eight weeks unless otherwise stated in the recipe, but it is actually literally unlikely you will ever have to worry about that.

Instructions for melting coconut and cacao butter are on page 86.

257

Star bar

Makes 36 squares
15 mins, 3 hrs setting
Blender

Be the star that you really are! This one's such a winner I wanted to make it into a bar, but the pollen doesn't keep well once it's ground up.

Melt the butter first. Grind the cacao in a high-power blender or food grinder, and remove. Put the gojis and pollen in the blender or grinder, and grind them up. Then add everything to the blender – melted butter, ground nibs, gojis and pollen, agave nectar, and purple corn extract. Blend again until you have a thick gloop. Pour into a large tray and leave in the fridge to set for three hours. When it's hard, cut into squares, six across by six down. Will keep for up to five days in the fridge.

200 g or 1½ cups coconut butter
150 g or 1½ cups cacao powder
150 g or 1½ cups gojis
150 g or 1½ cups pollen
3 tbsp agave nectar
2 tsp purple corn extract

Oh my goji

Serves 16
10 mins
Blender

I was trying to make a spread with gojis and coconut butter, but it wasn't working. So I added some chocolate powder, came up with this, and took it over to Lisa and Hector's house from Raw Gaia. That's one of the things about raw chocolate making – it's very, very hard to get it wrong, because even if it doesn't go to plan, it always ends up tasting the best ever.

Melt the coconut butter first, and once it's ready put all the ingredients in the blender together and blend until there are no chips of goji left and you have a thick cream. Pour into a small tray about 25 cm square and leave in the fridge for 3 hours to set. Once it is ready, cut into 16 squares.

150 g or 1¼ cups coconut butter
100 g or 1 cup gojis
3 tbsp agave nectar
150 g or 1½ cups cacao powder
50 g or ½ cup mesquite powder

Siriusly black

Makes 36 squares
10 mins, 3 hours setting
Blender

Etherium black and spirulina is a very grounding combination to keep you earthed and focused. I often use xylitol in raw chocolate recipes, it is made from fermented birch bark and is a natural sugar substitute. It is very sweet, so you only need about half the amount you would use of the powders like mesquite or lucuma. It is good to add when you need some extra sweetness but don't want to add anymore bulk to the recipe.

Melt the butter to start. Grind the nibs in a high-power blender or coffee grinder. Add the melted butter to the blender and blend again for a minute. Add in the remaining ingredients and blend one more time. Pour into a tray to set and leave in the fridge for three hours. Once it's set, pop out of the tray and cut into squares, six down by six across.

220 g or 1¾ cups coconut butter
250 g or 2 cups cacao nibs
100 g or 1 cup mesquite
50 g or ½ cup xylitol
1 tsp Etherium black
50 g or ½ cup Spirulina

Goco choco

Grinding up gojis into your chocolate mixtures makes amazing results. Gojis have a naturally healthy low-glycaemic sweetness which means you don't have to add so many powders and syrups to your chocolate mix. Coconut chips in chocolate are really beautiful; when you slice through the slab they make divine patterns.

Melt the butter first. Grind up the nibs with 50 g (½ cup) gojis in a high-power blender or grinder. When fully ground, add the butter and agave nectar and blend again for a minute. Once it's amalgamated, add the mesquite and Etherium red and blend one more time. Stir in the remaining 100 g (1 cup) gojis and the coconut chips by hand. I usually do this in the blender jug, but you can transfer to a bowl if you find it easier. Spoon into a tray and leave to set in the fridge for three hours. Once it's set, turn out and cut into squares, six across by six down. Will keep in the fridge for up to eight weeks.

220 g or 1¾ cups coconut butter
200 g or 1½ cups cacao nibs
150 g or 1½ cups gojis
150 g or 1½ cups mesquite
3 tbsp agave nectar
50 g or 1 cup coconut chips
1 tsp Etherium red

Pollen put the kettle on

Makes 36 squares
10 mins, 3 hours setting
No equipment needed

Mmm, mulberries. These sweet little Iranian berries are loved by everyone who comes across them; I don't know why they are not more readily available in this country. Sometimes they are quite crunchy, a bit like sugar puffs, but we like them best when they are moist and chewy and taste like honey. The softness of the mulberries contrasts beautifully with the crunchiness of the pollen. When we had the Raw Magic shop in 2006, mulberries and pollen was one of the most popular combinations.

Melt the coconut butter and cacao butter together. Cacao butter takes slightly longer to melt so put that in first. In a separate bowl put your cacao powder, lucuma and mesquite, and stir together. Pour in the melted butters and stir again. Finally, add the mulberries and pollen and give them a good mix in. Pour the mixture into a large tray and leave in the fridge to set for three hours. Once it's set, turn out and cut into cubes, six across by six down.

110 g or 1 cup coconut butter
110 g or 1 cup cacao butter
150 g or 1½ cups cacao powder
100 g or 1 cup lucuma
100 g or 1 cup mesquite
100 g or 1 cup mulberries
100 g or 1 cup bee pollen

Suma luvin

Makes 30 squares
10 mins, 3 hrs setting
No equipment needed

Suma can make you feel like you're floating on a fluffy cloud, and when you mix it with Etherium pink then it becomes a pink fluffy cloud and you feel like you are in love with yourself, your life, your world, the earth, the whole glorious lot of it.

250 g or 2 cups cacao butter
150 g or 1½ cups cacao powder
200 g or 2 cups mesquite
3 tbsp agave nectar
1 tsp Etherium pink
2 tsp suma

Melt the butter. Put all the other ingredients in another bowl and give them a good mix together. Pour in the melted butter and give another stir. Pour the chocolate into a large tray and leave in the fridge to set for three hours. When it's done, tip out and cut into cubes, six across by five down.

Everyone loves Linus

Makes 30 squares
15 mins, 3 hrs setting
Blender

Linus always puts mulberries in his chocolate so I had to name this one after him. For the record, can I say that it was me that introduced Linus to the wonders of cacao when I first moved to Brighton, and I think he's done an amazing job of taking the raw chocolate bar thing and really getting it out there into the mass market. RespecK.

230 g cacao butter
150 g mulberries
100 g mesquite
175 g cacao powder
5 drops orange oil
1 tsp Aulterra

To start, melt the cacao butter. Mash the mulberries in a grinder or food processor until they're a paste. Put all the ingredients together in the blender, and blend to a thick cream. Pour into a large tray and leave to set in the fridge for three hours. When it's hardened, pop it out and cut it into cubes, five across by six down.

Maca swirl

Makes 42 squares
10 mins, 3 hrs setting
No equipment needed

This is perhaps the most beautiful looking recipe in the chapter. The marble effect is easy to do and so professional looking. If you're a spirulina lover, you can make a green swirl by replacing the maca with spirulina.

Melt the coconut butter and cacao butter together. Cacao butter takes a little longer to melt, so put that in first. In a separate bowl, measure out the cacao powder, mesquite, maca and xylitol. Give them a good mix together, then pour in the butters and mix completely. In your heating bowl, heat the coconut butter for the swirl while you're mixing the chocolate. Then blend the butter, lucuma and maca in a bowl by hand. Pour half your chocolate into a large tray. Then pour some maca butter on top and swirl it around a bit so it's creating patterns in the chocolate. Pour some more chocolate on top, then some more maca and keep going until you've used all the chocolate, but you need to keep half the maca for the top. With the rest of the maca butter, swirl it over the top of the chocolate, creating artistic patterns. You can drag it with a knife to create lines like a fancy cake. Leave to set in the fridge for three hours. When it's set, cut into squares, seven across by six down. You will have gorgeous marble patterns running through the slab.

150 g or 1¼ cups coconut butter
100 g or 1 cup cacao butter
150 g or 1½ cups cacao powder
100 g or 1 cup mesquite
100 g or 1 cup maca
50 g or ½ cup xylitol

For the swirl:
100 g or ¾ cup coconut butter
80 g or ¾ cup lucuma
80 g or ¾ cup maca

Magic manna

How much magic can you mannage?

Makes 30 squares
15 mins, 3 hrs setting
Blender

220 g or 1¾ cups cacao butter
250 g or 2 cups cacao nibs
100 g or 1 cup mesquite
50 g or ½ cup lucuma
3 tbsp agave nectar
2 tbsp crystal manna

To start, melt the butter. Grind the nibs in a high-power blender or coffee-grinder. Add the melted butter and blend again until the butter and nibs have combined. Add the mesquite, lucuma, agave nectar, and blend one more time. Once you've got a runny chocolate cream, stir in one tablespoon of the crystal manna (stirring preserves the sparkly flakes visible in the chocolate). Pour half the chocolate into a medium-sized tray. Sprinkle the second tablespoon of crystal manna over the top in an even layer. Then pour the rest of the chocolate on top and leave it in the fridge to set. When it's ready, cut into cubes, five by six. You will have a thin line of green glitter running through the centre of your slab.

Minted

Makes 30 squares
10 mins, 3 hours setting
No equipment needed

Peppermint is one of the most popular flavours in chocolate. We find the best method for adding flavourings is with organic essential oils. These are the purest option, and you only need a few drops to get a really quality taste.

Melt the coconut butter and cacao butter together. In another bowl put the chocolate powder, mesquite, agave nectar, purple corn extract, crystal manna and peppermint. Give it all a good stir together, then pour in the melted butters and stir again. Add the raisins and coconut chips and give one final mix. Pour into a tray and leave in the fridge for three hours. When it's ready, turn it out and cut into cubes, five across by six down.

180 g or 1½ cups coconut butter
60 g or ½ cup cacao butter
175 g or 1¾ cups chocolate powder
200 g or 2 cups mesquite
3 tbsp agave nectar
1 tbsp purple corn extract
2 tbsp crystal manna
5 drops peppermint
100 g or 1 cup raisins
50 g or 1 cup coconut chips

Living lavender

Makes 30 squares
15 mins, 3 hrs setting
Blender

The quality of cacao butter available can be very variable.
If it's very cheap, it's probably not food quality, but used
for cosmetic use. It's not bad for you, but it won't have much taste. The best one we
have found by far is that sold by Detox Your World – the aroma is out of this world,
so enticing that many people just find themselves taking a bite straight off the block!
Plus an extra added bonus is that the containers they come in are *perfect* for using
as chocolate moulds.

150 g or 1¼ cups cacao butter
75 g or ½ cup coconut butter
250 g or 2 cups cacao nibs
100 g or 1 cup lucuma
100 g or agave nectar
1 tbsp purple corn extract
5 drops lavender

Melt the butters together. Grind the nibs
in a high-power blender or grinder. Put all
the ingredients together in the blender
and blend to a puree. Pour into a medium
sized tray and leave to set in the fridge for
three hours. Once it's set, turn it out, and
cut into squares, six across by five down.

B&B

Makes 30 squares
15 mins, 3 hrs setting
No equipment needed

Get some R&R with B&B – buckwheat and barberry – it's what Brighton's all about. He Shou Wu is a herb used in Chinese medicine that's become one of our favourite superfoods, it makes us feel on top of the world.

Melt the cacao butter and coconut butter together first. In a mixing bowl, stir together the chocolate powder, suma, and he shou wu. Stir in the melted butters and honey and give it another good mix. Finally stir in the buckwheaties and barberries and when they're evenly mixed in, pour it into a large tray and leave in the fridge to set for three hours. Once it's hard, turn it out and cut into cubes, five across by six down.

125 g or 1 cup cacao butter
50 g or ½ cup coconut butter
175 g or 1¾ cups chocolate powder
1 tbsp suma
1 tbsp he shou wu (recommended but optional)
120 g or ½ cup raw honey
100 g or 1 cup buckwheaties (p86)
50 g or ½ cup barberries

The grass is always greener

Makes 30 squares
15 mins, 3 hrs setting
No equipment needed

I love barleygrass in chocolate, it softens the stimulating effects of cacao and gives it a calmer, balanced, just plain greener edge. Yacon root is another aesthetically exciting addition to chocolate – it looks like yellow flowers in the grass, but maybe that's just me…

125 g or 1 cup coconut butter
125 g or 1 cup cacao butter
150 g or 1½ cups cacao powder
100 g or 1 cup mesquite
50 g or ½ cup barleygrass
50 g or ½ cup hemp protein powder
3 tbsp agave nectar
50 g or 1 cup yacon root

Melt the coconut butter and cacao butter together. In a mixing bowl stir together the cacao powder, mesquite, barleygrass and hemp protein powder so they're evenly mixed. Add the melted butters and agave nectar, and stir again. Finally stir the yacon root in thoroughly and pour into a large tray to set. After three hours, remove it from the tray and cut into squares, six across by five down.

Hi-flier

Makes 20 squares
10 mins, two hours setting
No equipment needed

This chocolate is not for the faint-hearted. Intense in flavour and effects, it will take you to places you didn't know it was possible to go with chocolate. One for the hardcore faithful, you know the score.

Melt the butter, and once it's ready add it to the rest of the ingredients. Give it a good stir and pour into a small tray. Once it's set, which should only take a couple of hours, turn out and cut into squares, four by five.

150 g or 1¼ cups cacao butter
175 g or 1¾ cups cacao powder
100 g or agave nectar
1 tsp blue manna
1 tsp Etherium gold

Blissful blue

What do you do when you're in love with someone who's not in love with you? You make some of this and remember that you are perfect, your pain and your love, all of it is perfect. You feed it to the person you love, and you set them free, you release yourselves from the patterns of pain and suffering you hold and you surrender to the knowledge of your own inner perfection, you trust in the rhythm of your own inner dance to take you to the places you need to go.

Melt the coconut butter first. Grind up the cacao nibs until they are completely powdered – if you're using whole vanilla pods it's best to grind them up with the nibs. Add the melted butter, cacao powder, mesquite, and xylitol in now, with the vanilla if it's not already in there, and give it another good blend. Measure

220 g or 1¾ cups coconut butter
150 g or 1¼ cups cacao nibs
75 g or ¾ cup cacao powder
150 g or 1½ cups mesquite
50 g or 1/3 cup xylitol
2 tsp blue manna
2 tbsp vanilla powder or 2 vanilla pods

in the blue manna and blend one last time. Pour into a large tray and leave in the fridge to set for three hours. Turn out and cut into cubes, five across by six down.

Hempster genes

Makes 25 squares
15 mins, 3 hrs setting
Blender

This is a bit fudgier than the other chocolates because it's made with hemp seeds rather than butter. Hemp and chocolate is a very grounding combination, the protein in the hemp and the kick in the cacao make this very strengthening and energising.

Blend the hemp seeds in a high-power blender or food grinder. Remove them from the machine, and then put the cacao nibs in and give them a good whiz. When they are completely broken down to a powder, add the hemp back in with the agave nectar, if you have a high-power blender. If not, transfer to a food processor and use that. You should end up with a sticky mass which you will need to remove with a spoon and press into a medium-sized tray. It should harden in about three hours. Cut into cubes, five by five. Will keep for up to two weeks in the fridge.

250 g or 2 cups hulled hemp seeds
250 g or 2 cups cacao nibs
4 tbsp agave nectar

Hi-five

Makes 30 squares
15 mins, 3 hrs setting
Blender

This was the first bar we made, along with the Hi-bar. I'm not a big eater of nuts, and the Hi-bar was made with brazil nuts, so I wanted to do a bar that was nut-free. We called this Hi-five because it contains five different types of seeds.

Grind the nibs in a high-power blender or coffee-grinder. Remove from the machine, and put in all the seeds together to grind them. Then if you're using a high-power blender, either put the cacao and seeds together in that, or transfer to a food processor. Add the agave nectar and give it a good mix until you have a sticky ball. Press into a tray and leave in the fridge to set. Once it's done, cut into squares, six down by five across. Will keep for up to two weeks in the fridge.

250 g or 2 cups cacao nibs
50 g or ½ cup hemp seeds
50 g or ½ cup pumpkin seeds
50 g or ½ cup sesame seeds
50 g or ½ cup sunflower seeds
50 g or 1/3 cup flaxseeds
3 tbsp agave nectar

Hi-seas

Makes 16 squares
10 mins, 2 hrs setting
Blender

Seaweed and chocolate seems an unlikely combination, and people either love this or hate this. I'm a big seaweed fan and I love this because I get to eat two of my favourite foods at once.

250 g or 2 cups cacao nibs
25 g or 1 cup dulse
60 ml or ½ cup hemp oil
120 ml or 1 cup agave nectar
1 tbsp kelp powder

Grind the nibs in a high-power blender or coffee grinder. Add the dulse and blend again until the dulse is completely powdered. Add the kelp, agave nectar and hemp oil and blend again until creamy. It's really good like this, warm and liquid straight from the blender. Press into a medium sized tray, and leave in the fridge to set for at least two hours. Once it's ready, turn out and cut into cubes, four across by four down.

Lucifari's chocolate halva

Makes 20 squares
15 mins, 3 hrs setting
Blender

We used to eat loads of Sunita halva, buy big 2.5 kg blocks and cane them. There's something so reassuring about the combination of sesame seeds and honey, and add some chocolate into the mix to find divine solace in this fudge. Ask Lucifer, he knows.

200 g or 2 cups sesame seeds
100 g or ½ cup honey
75 g or ¾ cup chocolate powder
1 tbsp vanilla powder or extract or 1 pod
50 g or ½ cup raisins

Grind the sesame seeds in a high-power blender or grinder; keep going until they're as mashed as you can get them. If you haven't got a high-power blender, transfer them to a food processor, and add the other ingredients. If you're using a high-power blender just add the honey, chocolate powder and vanilla. Give it a really good pounding until all the ingredients are as amalgamated as possible with as few traces of sesame seeds left as you can – just a ball of sticky fudge. Add the raisins in and give it a half-hearted go, so that they're still discernable in the mix. Spoon out into a medium sized tray and press down. Keep in the fridge for three hours, then turn out and cut into squares, four across by five down. Keep stored in the fridge for up to two weeks.

Basically, I'm spoiling you here: recipes are pretty superfluous when it comes to superfood drinks. Once you get into them, you'll realise that drinking them is by far the fastest, easiest and most effective way to get them into your system.

In teas, milks, or smoothies, superfood drinks will become an unmissable part of your daily intake. And here the possibilities really are limitless — just be guided by your intuition and use a little of everything you fancy. Gojis? Check. Lucuma? Check. Purple corn extract? Check. We never use teabags anymore, we just freestyle it with a teaspoon of this and a pinch of that.

No time for lunch? Throw your favourites in the blender with a generous serving of water, pour into a flask and take with you to drink on the go, it'll see you through easy until you have time to sit down for a big green salad.

Spiral tribe

Serves two
10 mins
Blender

Who'd have thought to name a smoothie after an early 1990's sound system that she used to squat with in South London? Oh, that'll be me. Spiral Tribe in the area, make some noise...

Quarter the pear, removing the stem and the pips. Peel the banana and break it into quarters. Put all the ingredients apart from the water in the blender and blend for a minute so the fruits are broken down. Then gradually add the water while the blender is turning.

1 pear
1 banana
1 tbsp Spirulina
2 dates
250 ml or 1 cup water

Macamilk

Thicker than water but thinner than a smoothie, my milks are really magic. By putting superfoods into water we help make them more absorbable, and their effects are stronger.

Serves two
5 mins
Blender

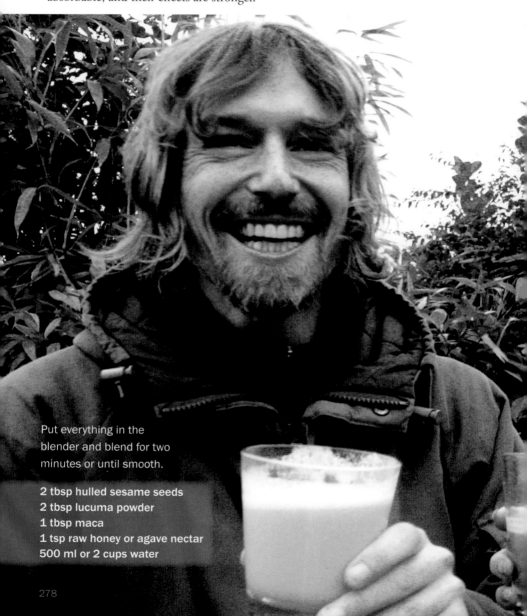

Put everything in the blender and blend for two minutes or until smooth.

2 tbsp hulled sesame seeds
2 tbsp lucuma powder
1 tbsp maca
1 tsp raw honey or agave nectar
500 ml or 2 cups water

Beat me up

Black and blue, this milk will slap you round the face a bit when you need waking up. In a very loving way, of course.

Serves one
5 mins
Blender

Put everything in the blender, adding the water gradually while the blender is turning. Blend for a minute until the cacao nibs are ground down.

1 tbsp cacao nibs
1 tbsp maca
1 tbsp lucuma
1 tsp xylitol
1/8 tsp Etherium black
¼ tsp blue manna
250 ml or 1 cup water

279

Barley blaster

This will turn you into a lean, green peace-making machine.

Serves two
5 mins
Blender

2 tbsp barleygrass
2 tbsp hulled hemp seeds
1 tsp cacao powder
¼ tsp purple corn extract
1 lemon, juiced
pinch salt
500 ml or 2 cups water

Put everything in the blender, with half of the water. Blend the lot up and gradually add the rest of the water. The result should be thinner than a smoothie, thicker than a milk. Drink immediately.

Milkalicious

Serves one
5 mins
Blender

Home-made milk doesn't come any easier. Just pop it in the blender and whizz for a minute. This works with most nuts and seeds, but hemp is our favourite for flavour and nutritional potency.

Blend. Um, that's it, really. Just blend.

2 tbsp hulled hemp seeds
250 ml or 1 cup water

Heaven's juice

How could you not lead a heavenly life when you can drink this every day?

Serves two
Blender
5 mins

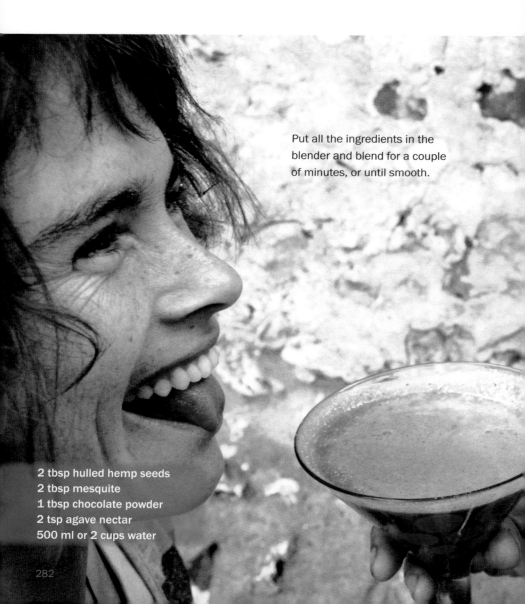

Put all the ingredients in the blender and blend for a couple of minutes, or until smooth.

2 tbsp hulled hemp seeds
2 tbsp mesquite
1 tbsp chocolate powder
2 tsp agave nectar
500 ml or 2 cups water

282

Purple passion milk

Serves one
5 mins
Blender

Who do you love? Write down the five people you know who inspire the most passion in you, and promise to share a glass of this juice with them all in the next week. Then write down five heroes and sheroes who you would love to have a purple passion party with and dream of it in the boring spaces when you're waiting for web pages to load or small children to finish on the toilet.

Put all your ingredients in the blender and blend for two minutes, or until smooth.

2 tbsp hulled hemp seeds
1 tsp purple corn extract
¼ tsp suma
1 tbsp raw honey or agave nectar
250 ml or 1 cup water

283

Camu get me

A bit like *Pudding it right* (p180) without the pudding.

Put everything apart from the water in the blender and give it a good whiz. Keep it turning and add the water gradually. Once it's all in, give it another 10 seconds and it'll be ready.

1 tbsp camu
50 g or ½ cup gojis
2 tbsp lucuma
1 tbsp agave nectar
1 lemon, juiced
25 g or ½ cup coconut chips
750 ml or 3 cups water

Goji orgasm

Serves one
5 mins
Blender

If you want to get cosmic, you have to stop worrying about the "hows" of life. Knowing what you want, focusing on the goals and just trusting in the universe to deliver, leaving the details to the divine intelligence to negotiate, creates space for the outrageous to happen and the universe to blow your mind. This smoothie will put you into that space where you don't care how, you just know, and that's the way it is.

60 g or 2/3 cup gojis
30 g or 1/3 cup almonds
30 g or 1/3 cup cacao nibs
400 ml or 1½ cups water

Put the gojis, almonds and nibs in the blender and add the water gradually, really slowly or it will end up bitty. Keep whizzing for a couple of minutes until it's smooth. Drink, and then make sure you've got lots to do, you'll be buzzing for hours.

My chocolate kingdom

Serves one
5 mins
Blender

It's an Edward Monkton card – "they brought me great MOUN-TAINS of CHOCOLATE and thereof I did eat. And it did not make me feel ILL or ASHAMED, neither did it put weight on my THIGHS. For the chocolate was health-giving and NOURISHING, and the more I ate, the more BEAUTIFUL I became." This man knows. Edward, if you're reading this, let us have your address and we'll send you some chocolate – maybe not a mountain but a generous amount, you know.

60 g or ½ cup macadamias
2 tbsp chocolate powder
1 tbsp mesquite
1 tbsp lucuma
1 tbsp xylitol
400 ml or 1½ cups water

Put everything except the water in the blender. Start off with half the water then add the rest in gradually, as the blender is turning. Blend for a few minutes until there are no lumps of nut left.

Perhaps he's perfect

Serves two
5 mins, pre-soaking 12 hrs
Blender

Yeah, you know, I really think he is. There's nothing about him I would change – the ups and the downs, when he's pushing me away, when he's pulling me close, when he's here, when he's gone, when we're alone, when we're at a party, when we're hanging out, when we're really hectic, when we're talking, when we're sitting in silence, when we're working, when we're playing, I love it all, all of the time.

2 tbsp almonds, soaked 12 hrs
2 tbsp bee pollen
2 tbsp gojis
2 tsp agave nectar
500 ml or 2 cups water

Pre-soak the almonds for at least one hour, preferably overnight. Put everything in the blender and add the water gradually, as the blender is running. Blend for two minutes, until there are no bits of almond left.

Macoffee

Serves one
2 mins
Kettle

Maca's malty taste lends itself well to hot drinks. If you are worried about overheating your maca with boiling water, just heat your water in a pan to the right temperature. Gives you a boost, just like coffee but with none of the downsides.

Put the maca, salt and agave nectar in a cup and add hot water.

> 1 tsp maca powder
> pinch crystal salt
> 1 tsp agave nectar
> 330 ml or 1 1/3 cups water

Witch's tea

Serves one
2 mins
Kettle

This purple and green brew is sure to cast a spell on everyone who drinks it.

Put the purple corn extract, algae, agave nectar and salt into a cup. Pour over just boiled, or not quite boiled water. If you are worried about heating your superfoods too much, heat the water in a pan to just the right temperature. This tea is quite strong, so you can make top-ups with it: when you've drunk half the cup, top up with more water, and do this every time until it's too diluted to drink anymore. You can usually get at least three top-ups from a cup.

> ½ tsp purple corn extract
> ¼ tsp blue-green algae
> 1 tsp agave nectar
> pinch salt
> 500 ml or 2 cups water

Wizard's tea

Serves one
Kettle
5 mins

This tea is warming, revitalizing, cleansing, and third-eye activating! What more could you want from a cuppa?

¼ tsp purple corn extract
¼ tsp dried chilli flakes
juice ¼ lemon
250 ml or 1 cup water

Boil the kettle! Put purple corn extract, chilli and lemon in cup and add hot water.

Mayan tea

Serves one
Kettle
2 mins

Chocolate was originally consumed by the Aztecs as a hot drink, mixed with vanilla and chilli.

½ tsp chocolate powder
¼ tsp dried chilli flakes
pinch salt
500 ml or 2 cups water

Put the powder, flakes and salt in a cup. Fill with boiled water. This is a strong drink, you can get a few top-ups out of it. When you've drunk half a cup, refill with hot water, and it will still taste good. You can usually do this three or four times before it starts getting too diluted.

Superbeing tea

Serves one
Kettle
5 mins

When you feel the world is a harsh and lonely place, make yourself a cup of this and feel re-inspired to enter the battle and fight for your right to live in the light.

Boil the kettle. Put everything in a cup and pour half the water in. When you've drunk half the tea, top it up with some more water – you can do this two or three times and it still tastes great.

1 tsp maca
½ tsp cacao
1 tsp lucuma
pinch salt
500 ml or 2 cups water

Go tea

Serves one
Kettle
5 mins

No, not a jazz-head beard, a tea to make you smile. Gojis in your tea is the best thing since… the gojis you had in your breakfast cereal, probably.

Boil the kettle. Put all the ingredients in the cup and pour the water in. Some of the gojis slurp into your mouth when you first start drinking, some get left at the bottom and get all plump and moist...

1 tbsp goji berries
½ tsp chocolate powder
1 tsp mesquite
pinch salt
250 ml or 1 cup water

When you first start to align yourself with magical ways of thinking, it can feel a bit lonely and strange. Often we doubt ourselves, and wonder if we are crazy to believe all these things when our programming and the information that we receive through the mainstream media and our families is telling us reality is such a different paradigm.

Here's a list of my favourite websites, most of which send out daily, weekly or monthly emails full of inspiration and cosmic reassurance. Life doesn't have to be a place of fear, suffering and confusion – it can be a place of joy, bliss and contentment, and regular reminders from people who are believing the dream and living this way can often change the way we feel about ourselves and our lives in that instant, and affect our thoughts and actions for the rest of the day.

http://www.crystalinks.com/

The cosmic encyclopedia, with all the answers to all the questions you never even knew to ask.

http://www.tut.com/

Notes from the universe, daily uplifting emails to keep us aligned with our universal purpose.

http://www.treeofthegoldenlight.com/

Channelings from ascended masters and the galactic federation.

http://www.diagnosis2012.co.uk/

2012, coming your way soon. What does it mean? This site has all the answers.

http://www.cygnus-books.co.uk/

The UK's best spiritual bookstore.

http://www.infinitebeing.com/

Weekly emails on the shift in consciousness and what that means for humanity.

http://www.whatsuponplanetearth.com/

Messages from the higher realms, helping us understand the changes we are going through.

http://www.matthewbooks.com/

Matthew channels through his mother, information on life on earth and in heaven.

http://www.livingmagically.co.uk/

Gill Edwards' beautiful site on creating heaven on earth.

http://www.spiritlite.com/

Channeled messages through Dr Meg Blackburn Losey.

http://www.kachina.net/~alunajoy/

Center of the Sun – Mayan inspiration from Aluna Joy Yax'kin.

http://www.maryrobinsonreynolds.com/

Motivational and inspirational email updates and online movies.

Books

Eat Smart, Eat Raw by Kate Wood

Raw Living by Kate Wood

Ecstatic Beings by Kate Magic & Shazzie

Detox your World by Shazzie

Naked Chocolate by Shazzie & David Wolfe

Maca by Beth Ley

Wild Blue-Green Algae by Gillian McKeith

Primordial Food by Christian Drapeau

The Healing Powers of Pollen by Patrice Percie du Sert

Seven Health Secrets from the Hive by Charles H. Robson

The Wheatgrass Book by Anne Wigmore

Fats that Heal, Fats that Kill by Udo Erasmus

Messages from Water by Masaru Emoto

Living Magically by Gill Edwards

Excuse me, Your Life is Waiting by Lynne Grabhorn

The Power of Now by Ekhart Tolle

Be Here Now by Ram Dass

The Field by Lynne McTaggart

Anastasia Chronicles by Vladimir Megre

Love without End, Jesus Speaks by Glenda Green

Websites

www.newstarget.com
www.bestdayever.com
www.rawinspirations.com

Shopping

www.rawliving.eu
www.detoxyourworld.com
www.sunfood.com

Make Magic Happen!

Kate Magic Wood is now offering the most exciting raw training days ever! Make Magic Happen – in your kitchen, in your life and in the world. Learn how easy it is to be a gourmet raw chef, and how tuning into your body's cellular wisdom with raw foods creates more love and simplicity in your life and activates your own inner magic.

It's never been easier to take your destiny into your own hands, improve your life and the lives of your loved ones, and create the happiness revolution we all deserve. We can live together in love, peace and unity, and we have all the tools to make it happen. Are you ready? Then read on....

One of my favourite sayings is, "Why should the glass be half full or half empty? Why can't it just be full?" I believe that we are at a point in human history where we are fast-tracking into a new phase of evolution, a quantum leap where we know and experience that everything is possible and we achieve the miraculous on a daily basis. Sure, there are way too many awful things happening in the world today, but I passionately believe the way to change them is to *be the change!* "With our thoughts we make the world," said the Buddha, so if we change our consciousness we can change our reality.

There are many paths to the place of divine inner bliss and alignment, and raw foods and superfoods is one of the most powerful. By eating a diet as untampered with and unprocessed as possible, by cleansing on a deep cellular level and altering our energetic blueprint, by feeding ourselves the most mineral rich, nutritionally dynamic, mind expanding foods available on this planet, we start gaining a life more abundant than we have ever dreamed, more fulfilling than we ever knew possible.

"I have to say she is amazing, has completely transformed my life. Not only did I lose over 2 stone without trying, she has taught me how to make the most magical foods in no time, foods that empower me on physical & consciousness-expansion levels to enable me to keep up with my insane lifestyle, with ease! Chocolate cake for breakfast anyone?!"

Rochelle Vincente • www.myspace.com/product01

So come and hang out with me for a day in my idyllic home in central Brighton*. We'll talk about whatever you want – your life, my life, and I'll answer all your burning questions from, "How long should I soak my buckwheat?" to "What do you think is really going to happen in 2012?"

I'll share with you my knowledge and insights gained from over 14 years on a raw diet, and other holistic lifestyle tips to make it easy for you. I'll talk a lot about love, and the power of positive energy to create magic in our lives.

And of course, we'll make the best food ever! Soups, dips, salads, cakes, puddings, chocolates, sweets, loads to eat and more to take home with you. We'll spend hours playing with superfoods in the kitchen, so you'll go home feeling like a true alchemist. I am one of the most experienced raw chefs in the world, and an expert in whipping up gourmet style food with the minimum of fuss and hassle. My meals are so nutritionally packed, so vibrantly alive, so downright exciting to eat, and I can teach you how easy it is to make it yourself, and eat this way every day.

A Make Magic Happen day lasts for five hours, including food and books to take home and an initial fifteen minute telephone consultation with Kate. To book, go to www.rawliving.eu.

If you prefer, Kate can come to you for a small extra charge.

"Had some of Kate's Be the Change chocolate on Christmas Day. I think Kate is the change! She understands the things that are going on in this world and remains so full of love and lightness and goodwill to everyone."
Holly Paige • www.rawcuisine.co.uk